THE
UNKNOWN
FOREST

THE
UNKNOWN FOREST

A Walker's Guide to the New Forest

Anne-Marie Edwards

COUNTRYSIDE BOOKS
NEWBURY BERKSHIRE

First Published 1981
© Anne-Marie Edwards 1981
Reprinted 1983

COUNTRYSIDE BOOKS
3, Catherine Road
Newbury, Berkshire

ISBN 0 905392 08 6

Designed by Mon Mohan

Cover photographs by Derek Joseph

Printed in England by
J. W. Arrowsmith Ltd., Bristol

Typeset by Datchet Printing Services
Datchet, Berkshire

For Charlie

Acknowledgements

I am grateful to all the people who have helped me on my travels, the Forestry Commission, the Ramblers Association, Hythe, Totton and Southampton Public libraries for their unfailing assistance, and all my friends for their encouragement. Quotations from 'Hampshire Days', 'Remarks on Forest Scenery', 'Rural Rides', and 'It Happened in Hampshire' are by kind permission of the publishers. Grateful thanks finally to my daughter Julie, who accompanied me on my walks, drew the sketch maps and typed the manuscript, and my husband Mike who looks after me.

Contents

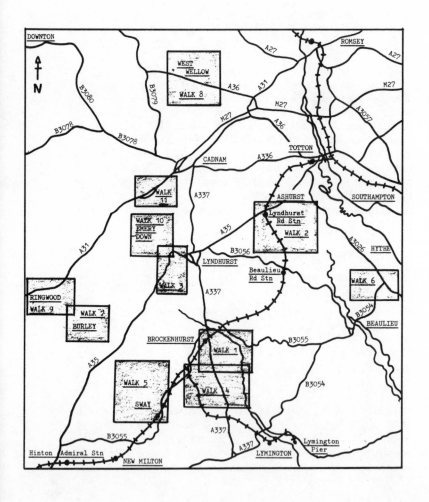

Getting to know
the Forest

There is nowhere else like the New Forest in the world. By some miracle the oldest and largest medieval Forest in Europe has survived here, in the crowded south of England, just over an hour's train ride from London. And, even more surprising, most of its glorious wilderness is very little known. A few minutes walk from the noisy centres or one of the many car parks sited along the roads and the real New Forest is waiting for you to discover it. Silent, delightful, and with an incredible richness of scenery and wildlife; you will find it is a magical Forest — this Forest so few people know. But it only gives up its secrets to those on foot.

The Forest can be misleading. There are too many paths, all of them tempting; there are no signposts and one wood can look very much like another. If you have left a car, you must get back to it! So I have devised this book as a series of safe family walks, all roughly circular, with starting points accessible by car and public transport. They are not the frequented ways, but my own favourite walks; each of them showing a different aspect of the Forest's beauty or its history. I hope you will try them and discover for yourself the magic of the real Forest, hidden from the crowds.

You will be making a journey in time. The Forest is little changed for all its nine hundred years of history. For it was in 1079 that William the Conqueror declared the wilderness of Ytene, named after the Jutes who settled here early in the fifth century, to be his own hunting ground; his 'New Forest'. The heaths and woodlands then extended north from the Solent shore to the Wiltshire Downs and west from Southampton Water to the Avon valley. All this was now to be 'afforested'; subject to the harsh Norman Forest law. The red deer were to roam unmolested to provide sport for the King and his friends. No other man could hunt or farm in the 'New Forest' or enclose any part of the land. The Saxons were left in no doubt about the King's ownership, the name 'Forest' meant it was royal property. It still is today. And if William was to jump on his horse and come riding through the Forest glades now, he would find his way without much difficulty, essentially it has remained the same. He would be surprised to see large herds of fallow deer instead of red, and he might wonder where the wolves and wild boar had gone. The pine trees would also surprise him as these were only introduced in large numbers into the Forest in the mid-nineteenth century. He would not be able to ride so far. Forest villages have expanded and farms encroached upon the boundaries. But still today, over a hundred square miles of this unique Forest remain, managed by the Forestry Commission and, by custom, open for us all to enjoy.

There is so much in the Forest to delight you. But I think its greatest glory is what the Commission term the 'ancient and ornamental' woodlands. These are the oldest woods of oak and beech trees, many of them cut short, or pollarded at an early period of growth. As this custom was declared illegal in 1698, many of these great trees must be up to four hundred years old. Without their heads, their main trunks have sprouted several stems which now, wreathed with ivy and often set with little gardens of ferns, spread massive arms far over the Forest floor. In the past the pollards were useful as well as beautiful, the curved branches provided just the right shaped 'knees' and 'elbows' for the shipbuilders at Forest ports like Lymington and Bucklers Hard. If you visit the old cottage at Furzey Gardens, near Minstead, you will see old tarred ship's timbers used as building material.

Now we simply enjoy their natural beauty: the intricate patterns of their branches black against the winter sky, the subtle shading of green revealed in Spring sunlight, the deep russet red of last year's leaves beneath the beeches. These woods, particularly where oaks predominate, are loved by all wild creatures. You will see fallow deer with their spreading antlers, the smaller reddish-brown roe, the little spotted sika and if you are lucky, a massive red deer stag guarding his harem of hinds with their floppy ears and large eloquent eyes. Kingfishers gleam over the Forest streams, herons stalk the marshes, the large green and red woodpeckers tap insistently for termites against dead stumps, their calls echoing like laughter round the woods.

Out on the heath too, there are sounds and scents to haunt your memory: larks soaring and singing even on grey days, heather and gorse smelling as rich as honey, the sharp tang of the gold-withey (or bog myrtle) as you brush past it by the streams. You will be rewarded by spreading views, west over the Avon valley to the Wiltshire Downs, south to the curving line of the Isle of Wight hills. And here you will feel close to the Forest's history as you pass tumuli or burial mounds raised by Britons a thousand years before the birth of Christ, and climb the embankments of Iron Age hill forts which dominated the hill tops when the Romans landed.

And you will discover the meaning of the law of the Forest. In order to survive, the people who lived close to the Forest had to be granted certain rights. They were allowed to pasture their ponies, cattle, donkeys and geese in the Forest, and, during the pannage season in Autumn when the acorns and beech seeds (mast) had fallen, they could turn out their pigs. Other rights included permission to gather firewood, cut peat, and spread marl dug from pits in the Forest to improve the quality of their land. These rights were attached to certain houses. Today, the people who live in those houses, the Commoners, exercise their rights as vigorously as ever. They own the famous ponies, rounding them up at various times of the year for marking and sale with scenes reminiscent of the Wild West. For these tough, shaggy ponies, only found in the New Forest, have not forgotten their wild ancestry. They look docile but, like any wild creature, head for cover the moment they suspect their freedom is threatened. Their tempers too are uncertain and it is dangerous, however appealing they look, to feed them.

If you buy or rent a house in the Forest, you can check whether you have 'rights of common' in an atlas kept in the office of the Clerk to the verderers in Lymington. The verderers are officials of the ancient Forest court, still meeting regularly to settle local differences in the original courthouse in Lyndhurst, the Forest capital. The court is open to all and well worth a visit.

I have planned the walks to reveal all these varied aspects of the Forest. It is a voyage of discovery. We follow a ridgeway deep into the great woods around Lyndhurst, take a smuggler's track to an ancient hill fort at Burley, come across Gritnam, a tiny hamlet in a Forest clearing that could have arrived straight out of the Domesday Book, and visit Castle Malwood where William the Conqueror's favourite son, William Rufus, feasted the night before his fatal hunting expedition.

The Forest is quiet now, possibly quieter than at any other time in its long history. In the past we would meet the people who lived and worked here, all dependent to some extent, on the Forest. We would meet gypsies, charcoal-burners, woodcutters, snake-catchers, swineherds, perhaps even smugglers! They have all gone yet the Forest holds their story still. As we walk, we hear some of that story, and other more strange tales from the Forest's wealth of folklore.

Now some practical advice. For most of the year, you will need strong, waterproof shoes as however dry the Forest may look, there is sure to be a boggy patch lurking somewhere. When the Forest is very wet, boots with Vibram soles will give a better grip than wellies. Forest bogs, identifiable from a distance by waving tufts of cotton grass, are best avoided even if it may mean a detour. If in doubt, keep to the heather, or ground under trees, and look for an animal track round them; deer don't like getting their feet wet. There is no need to worry about snakes. There are adders (V-markings down their backs) but they are much more terrified of you than you are of them and will quickly get out of your way. If you, or your dog, are unfortunate enough to be bitten, contact the local hospital, Southampton or Lymington, immediately. They stock anti-snake serum.

The Forest is a labyrinth of paths and it is unwise to ramble without a good map. Here I must add that my maps are only sketch maps, designed to assist you in reaching the start of each walk and to give an overall view of the route to be covered. If you wish to refer to proper maps I would advise purchasing the Ordnance Survey Tourist Map for the New Forest, or the excellent Outdoor Leisure Map now available. (Scale 1:25000 or about $2\frac{1}{2}$ inches to 1 mile.)

Other useful items I pack in my bag are a snack — chocolate and fruit — and a pair of warm gloves. I hope you will feel tempted to try these walks and rediscover this wonderful part of our heritage. Of one thing you can be sure. However often you

12

may walk even a familiar way, you will never tire of the New Forest. With its changing colours, its hazy, shimmering distances, its dappled effects of light and shade, it is never the same from one day to the next. The Forest remains a continually unfolding source of delight.

Note: Although we can wander freely in the Forest, the Forestry Commission has a duty to make it pay its way. So protect our good name and the national interest by shutting all gates and avoiding any risk of fire. Outside the Forest boundaries, every care has been taken to follow rights of way or paths to which the public has been granted access. However, these are liable to change for which the author cannot be held responsible.

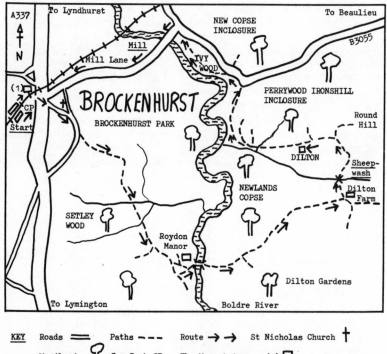

A337
N

To Lyndhurst
To Beaulieu
B3055

NEW COPSE
INCLOSURE

Mill
Mill Lane
IVY
WOOD

(1)
CP
Start

BROCKENHURST

BROCKENHURST PARK

PERRYWOOD IRONSHILL
INCLOSURE

Round
Hill

DILTON

Sheep-
wash

NEWLANDS
COPSE

Dilton
Farm

SETLEY
WOOD

Roydon
Manor

Dilton Gardens

To Lymington

Boldre River

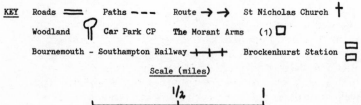

Brockenhurst and the Boldre River: In the steps of Brusher Mills and W H Hudson

This is a fascinating and unusual ramble. We see some of the most beautiful Foreset countryside as we walk through great woods of beech and oak. But we also see some of the more hidden delights of the Forest which contribute to its magic. We visit the oldest church in the Forest where there is a carving of a famous snake-catcher, Brusher Mills, and explore one of the great parks surrounding what was in former times a powerful manor. Few people knew the Forest as well as W H Hudson, the naturalist, or wrote about it with greater perception. We pass Roydon Manor which he described in his delightful book 'Hampshire Days', and follow in his footsteps beside the Boldre river.

Our starting point is Brockenhurst Station. The distance round is about six miles, but allow a whole morning or afternoon for this walk as there is much to see.

From the Station, walk towards the crossing over the A337, past the Morant Arms. Cross the line and walk a few yards along the main road in the direction of Lymington. On the left you pass Mill Lane, the B3055 to Beaulieu (we come down Mill Lane to join the main road here at the end of our walk). A little further on you come to a second, smaller road on the left signposted to St Nicholas Parish Church. Follow this narrow lane as it curves uphill between high hedges spiked with blackthorn and twisting sprays of honeysuckle.

BROCKENHURST CHURCH (see Note 1), like all Forest churches, stands on top of the hill to serve as a landmark for travellers. It dates back to Saxon times and is full of interest.

After a good look round inside I walked down the hill to the east side of the churchyard to see the beautifully kept memorial to the New Zealand and Indian soldiers who lie there. Brockenhurst played its part in both world wars; during the first it was the home of a base hospital.

I then had another look at the headstone of a local Forest personality, BRUSHER MILLS (see Note 2). His grave is in the north-east corner of the churchyard and you will recognise it by the carving of Brusher on the stone holding his snakes.

From the Church, follow the road as it bears right. Past the corner you will see a footpath leading from the road on the left, opposite a farm entrance. It is marked as a bridleway. Go through the gate and follow this footpath, bordered with ancient oaks running along the southern edge of Brockenhurst Park. This is part of the land belonging to BROCKENHURST MANOR (see Note 3) which once stood here whose history, like that of the church, can be traced to the Domesday Book.

Our path crosses a wide, grassy avenue. This is known as 'The Gallops' and was the training ground of 'Lovely Cottage' the Grand National winner. Go through a wicket gate and along the edge of a wood, keeping the trees close on your right. The path leaves the farmland to wind downhill through Setley Wood. As I walked under the young oaks and beeches the air was noisy with the calls of rooks and pigeons. Our path comes down to a stream, over a bridge, then up through a gap in the old Inclosure boundary to cross an open glade dotted with silver birches and willows. We cross another stream and climb uphill where you will see farmland again through the trees on your left. A wider track joins ours. Bear left for a short distance along this track until on the left you see the lodge by a private road to Roydon Manor. Follow the footpath sign straight on until you see another white gate on the left. This one is marked 'Private Woods, bridlepath only' and leads to a right of way. Turn left, through the gate, and follow this path past Roydon Manor to cross the Boldre river into Newlands Copse.

As we pass this lovely seventeenth century house I must introduce another fascinating person who loved the Forest, W H Hudson. He came to live at ROYDON MANOR (see Note 4) at the turn of this century. Perhaps better known as the author of 'Green Mansions', he was passionately interested in wildlife, making his own observations of his surroundings which he records in his book 'Hampshire Days'.

Below the Manor, we cross the Boldre — or Lymington — river by a wooden footbridge. Looking at the water, it is exactly as W H Hudson describes it, the colour of old sherry! Climb through the wood and walk along the edge of Newlands Copse. Follow the track over farmland to Dilton Farm. Just before the farm turn left and follow the path over the meadows aiming for the corner of Beaulieu Heath, south of Round Hill. On the way you cross a small stream and here, Bill Johnson, a local farmer, showed me the remains of a sheepwash. Below the right hand side of the bridge is a circular, brick enclosure with a small exit, which could be temporarily barred. Bill explained that disinfectant was put in the pool and the sheep thoroughly dipped in it before being allowed out of the narrow exit into the stream where they were helped ashore onto a pebble beach. You can imagine the busy, noisy scene on a warm June day! Today all is quiet and deserted but the rise beyond the stream is still called Sheepwash Hill. Keep straight on, through the gate onto the heath.

From the gate, turn left along one of the concrete tracks that remain from the air base built here during the last war. Walk for a short distance along the concrete until you come to a gravel track bearing slightly right, downhill, marked 'No through road, Dilton only'. Take this track to leave the bleakness of the heath behind and walk along a green valley with the scattered cottages that comprise Dilton on your left. Cross the stream and walk on into the wood ahead. Keeping the stream on your left, follow the track through Perrywood Ironshill Inclosure, a beautiful oak and beech wood with wide, mossy glades. At a fork, bear left towards the western edge of the Inclosure. All around me, squirrels were busily hunting up last year's nuts and birds rose in fluttering whirls, calling shrilly at my intrusion. Two magpies flapped noisily away from me. Once these smart birds were rare in the Forest, but they are now back in large numbers. They were a favourite bird of the gypsies who used to keep them as pets. Our track now becomes deeply rutted and runs close to the boundary fence. Beyond the fence, on the left, the ground falls away to give glimpses of the Boldre river. The woods thin, and we leave the Inclosure to cross a green lawn. Go through the gate ahead to the B3055 the road from Brockenhurst to Beaulieu. Turn left and follow the road towards Brockenhurst. Cross a stream, then look to the left of the road for the car park and picnic area, Ivy Wood. Turn left, and walk across the car park to the Boldre river. Turn right and follow the bank of the stream to a bridge with white railings. Rejoin the road, and turn left over the bridge. The old mill is on the right and you can see traces of the former workings. You pass impressive park gates, a reminder that you are now skirting the northern edge of Brockenhurst Park. Opposite the gates is a cottage with a large 'M' for Morant above the door. The railway is over the fields to the right and after about half a mile you will see Brockenhurst Station ahead. Leave the B3055, Mill Lane and turn right to cross the main road back to the station.

Notes for Walk 1

Note 1 *Brockenhurst Church*
The Parish Church of Saint Nicholas at Brockenhurst is the most ancient in the New Forest. There was a Saxon church here (some Saxon herring bone masonry will be found in the lower part of the wall between the south doorway and the east end of the Nave) and the Domesday book records the existence of a church at 'Broceste' which is how the Norman scribes spelled the name of the village. The oldest part of the present building dates from the twelfth century. The south doorway with its lovely semicircular arch, chevron mouldings and scalloped capitals shows Norman work at its best. The font, a lead-lined bowl of Purbeck stone, is also Norman. Among many other interesting features is a charming, curtained 'Squire's pew', like a small boxed-in room with seats all round. It is easy to imagine Addison's Sir Roger de Coverley, sleeping peacefully through the sermon in such delightful seclusion!

As you approach the south porch, on the left is an enormous yew. The creased and pleated trunk measures fifteen feet round. It deserves its mention in the Domesday Book.

Note 2 *Brusher Mills*
Brusher was what the Romanies call a sap engro — a snake catcher. He was called Brusher because another of his occupations was to sweep the loose snow off the ice on Brockenhurst pond for skaters. But he made his living from the adders he caught in the Forest. C J Cornish, writing about the Forest in 1894 describes Brusher as 'a strikingly handsome man slung all over with bags of sacking ... from his chest hangs a

18

pair of long steel forceps. He carried a light stick with a ferrule, into which when he rouses a snake he puts a short forked piece of hazel wood and darting it forward with unerring aim, pins the adder to the ground. Stooping down he picks it up lightly with the forceps and transfers it to his sack'. The ointment made from adder fat was good for 'sprains, black eyes, poisoning with brass, bites by rats and horses, rheumatic joints and sore feet in men and dogs'. He loved animals and cared for any sick ones he found. As a sideline he would sit by the road and entertain travellers on their way to Bournemouth with the snakes he kept in his pocket. His headstone shows him holding a handful of lively-looking snakes outside his Forest home, which, like the charcoal burners' huts, was a simple wigwam of branches covered with turf. One evening he returned home to find his hut destroyed by vandals. It is said that this so upset him that he became ill and died shortly afterwards, but he will never be forgotten; he has become part of Forest folklore.

Note 3 *Brockenhurst Manor*

In Norman times the Lord of this Manor enjoyed many privileges. He could retain his land and exercise his rights of common to graze his animals and gather fuel, in the words of Domesday, 'quit and free from Verderers and foresters without hindrance from the King'. But conditions were attached. During the reign of Henry II, the Lord of the Manor, William Spilman, was required to entertain the King when he came hunting. His son, also William, was required to serve the King for eleven days in the event of war. A branch of the most recent holders of the Manor, the Morant family, still lives in the area but the old Manor itself has been pulled down. A charming publication by the WI 'It Happened in Hampshire' tells us that in 1812 a Dame's School was established in Brockenhurst by Lady Caroline Morant. Miss Ash, a lame girl of eighteen, from London, was installed as Headmistress in one of the largest cottages where, for fifty years, she ruled with a rod of iron. On Sundays she accompanied her scholars to church in her donkey cart, the girls in uniform made by themselves from material provided by Lady Caroline, with muslin scarves and straw bonnets tied with pink and white checked ribbon. Every year they visited the Park for the school treat. At the head of the children's procession rode Miss Ash, the donkey dressed fore and aft in thick white cotton trousers tied with blue and yellow ribbons, the Morant colours! A former scholar of this severe lady reports that the girls had their aprons pinned to Miss Ash's and were made to kneel upright. The game was to fall over thus ripping off the teacher's apron! They evidently had a lively sense of mischief like one naughty boy who, locked as a punishment in a dark outhouse, discovered a store of apples in a corner. He took just one bite out of every apple!

Note 4 *Roydon Manor*

Originally this was a Manor House, but when W H Hudson lived here in 1902 it had been turned into a farm. He notes the date of the house, 1692, cut in a stone tablet in one of the rooms. Today the house has been restored from the rather ramshackle state he describes in 'Hampshire Days' but still looks very much as he pictures it: 'never have I known any human habitation, in a land where people are discovered dwelling in so many secret, green, out of the world places, which has so much of nature in and about it ... a small old picturesque red-brick house with high pitched roof and tall chimneys, a great part of it overrun with ivy and creepers, the walls and roof stained by time and many-coloured lichen to a richly variegated greyish red'. By his front door, he writes, 'a tiny gold crested wren sat on her eggs in her little cradle nest suspended to a spray of yew'. Small insects fascinated him. Observing that female grasshoppers were often ignored by the males and often sat patiently alone for hours, he carried one into the house on a wild rose branch. There she remained for sixteen days. When she had eaten all the berries on her branch, he kept her alive with a varied diet which included bread and butter pudding and ginger beer!

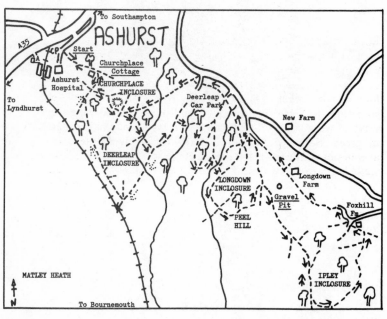

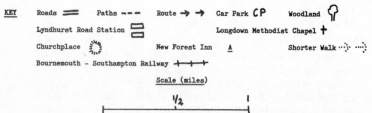

Border Country:
The North East Terraces

Border country is always fascinating. This walk takes you along the north-east boundary of the Forest where there is an almost startling contrast between the Forest, so much a world of its own, and the farming land it adjoins. The land is high, and looking the other way, over the Forest from paths that sometimes follow terraces along the hillsides, you see wave after wave of woodland rolling westward in every imaginable shade of green. Some of the woods here are newly planted with avenues of young trees that just meet over your head so that you walk beneath them feeling like Gulliver. Allow at least four hours for this walk, a little over eight miles round. If you can spare a full day you will be able to allow yourself more 'time to stand and stare'. But I also suggest an optional shorter route of about three miles. The starting point is Ashurst village, Lyndhurst Road Station if you arrive by train.

We begin from the village car park. If you are driving from Southampton turn left before the railway bridge and you will see the park just past Ashurst Hospital gates. From the station, turn right and cross the bridge, then right again into the car park. Stand with your back to the park and the Hospital on your right, and you will see a wide gravel track running behind the Hospital towards Churchplace Inclosure. This is our way. The white buildings of the Hospital were once the New Forest Union workhouse. To the left of the track towards the cricket ground used to be some fine trees, survivors of what were once dense woods fringing a forest lawn. The lawn stretched beside the Southampton road for two miles. One of the first writers to describe the Forest, William Gilpin, noted in 1790:

'The name of this beautiful and extensive forest scene is Hounsdown; so named probably from the fair advantage it gives the hound in pursuit. If he can drive his chase, from the thickets into this open plain, it is probable he will there secure him.' This area is still called Hounsdown today and nearby is Hunter's Inn hill.

Follow the track past a notice 'Churchplace Cottage only' until you come to this attractive forest lodge on your right. Turn right through a gate into the Churchplace Inclosure. The keeper's house was built the same time as the woods were planted — 1810 — as an inscription over a window of the cottage indicates. Squirrels revel in these woods of young oaks and beeches. They scamper across your path rustling the dead leaves, skim up the tree trunks to pause spreadeagled if they suspect you have seen them, and leap from branch to branch above your head. Look for woodpeckers too, particularly the brilliantly coloured large green bird with his strange 'laughing' call.

When you come to a crosspath, turn left along the gravel track. The track rises a little and then bears right past a knoll crowned with much older beeches. This is CHURCHPLACE (see Note 1), possibly the site of one of the Saxon churches William the Conqueror was said to have destroyed when he declared the New Forest his exclusive hunting reserve in 1079.

Follow the track as it bears right to a cross path. Now keep straight ahead down the gravel track opposite. Dark pines cast heavy shade over your path. On the right is Deerleap Inclosure. Gilpin explains this Forest name: 'Here a stag was once shot; which in the agony of death, collecting his force, gave a bound, which astonished those who saw it. It was immediately commemorated by two posts, which were fixed at the two extremities of the leap, where they still remain. The space between them is somewhat more than eighteen yards.'

You soon come to another crosstrack. Keep straight on down the green ride ahead. Now you are really in the still heart of the pinewoods, walking on a delicious soft and scented carpet of emerald moss. Walk down to a bridge over a tiny tributary of the Beaulieu river then up the opposite slope to a gate. Go through the gate into a different world! You are now standing on the open windswept heath dotted with a handful of gnarled Scots pines. (For the shorter walk, about four miles round, turn right to the bridge over the railway. Just before the bridge, turn right again and return at first close to the line, then, keeping to the same track, through Churchplace Inclosure). To continue on our present route, turn left from the gate opening onto the heath. Ignore the tempting gates into Longdown Inclosure opposite, and walk over the heath to a second pair of double gates into the Inclosure. Turn right through the gates into Longdown. These are the new woods I mentioned. The pines were planted in the 1960's and as our path is wide and open, we can see over the tops of them, west across the Forest. After crossing a stream, the path climbs and the gravel gives way to grass. Take the first track you meet on the right. This hugs the hillside so that you follow a wide terrace with a valley rippling with young pines beside you. Go straight over a crosstrack, following the path as it bears left. When you come to a gravel track, turn right onto it and follow it downhill to cross a stream. Our way now becomes a green ride and bears right towards Peel Hill. Keep to the ride, straight over a gravel track, to the eastern edge of Longdown Inclosure. Look back for a moment west, over the woods and heath each side of the Beaulieu river, across the great trees of Matley to see Lyndhurst church spire against the skyline — a solitary marker in what appears a wilderness of forest. Go through the double gates onto the heath. Ignore the track on the right which goes down to the river and follow the path ahead which winds a little right over the heath towards a dark cluster of Scots pines. This is Ipley wood — our destination. Walk under the pines and over smooth green lawns to the gate into the wood. This is the ideal place for a rest and a snack. Just visible through the trees on the left is a track which leads through Marchwood to CRACKNORE HARD on Southampton Water (see Note 2).

Walk on into Ipley wood through the double gates. This is also newly planted and our track leads down to the southern edge of the wood, where you can see across the heath far over the Beaulieu river, then round in a semi-circle to the northern edge of the wood. Here we turn for home. Go through the gate and turn left in the direction of Lyndhurst Road Station (Ashurst village). Walk along the northern limit of Ipley wood, with the trees on your left. Our return route is a direct one — about three and a half miles from this point. We are now following the line of the Forest boundary over a kind of no-mans-land of green lawns alive with rabbits! It's interesting to compare the long silent line of dark Forest trees on the left with the farming land on the right dotted with neat houses beside tidily hedged fields. When you come to a crosstrack with a path leading left into the wood, look for a farm gate on the right. Turn right through the gate, then immediately left — heading as before — to cross a plank bridge. Keep straight on, uphill, towards the line of a gravel pit ahead. Aim to leave the pit on your left. The track narrows to lead you past the pit through a copse of fine old oak trees. Pass Longdown Farm on your right and follow the track until it meets a narrow tarmac road. Walk down the road for a short distance until you see Longdown Methodist Chapel on your left. Turn left down the little path to the right of the chapel, past the Forestry Commission barrier. Ahead is a gate into the Inclosure but just before you reach it, a little track winds away downhill to your right. Take this track for a few yards keeping the Inclosure boundary fence on your left to join a wide gravel track leading straight ahead in our direction. This leads us over a stream then ends as abruptly as it began! However a narrow path leads us straight on through the gorse bushes, over a small hill to another wide track. Follow this over the heath to the edge of Churchplace Inclosure. Here our way is interrupted by Deerleap Car Park. Walk straight across the park to the point where a lane leads right to join the road. Our way is the broad green track you see straight ahead. It is barred to prevent motor access, but it is a simple matter for us to cross the cattle grid and pick our way left to join it. Now for a little careful navigation! Follow this wide way for about a hundred yards and just before the top of a slight rise look for a gate on your left leading into Churchplace Inclosure. Turn left through the gate into the Inclosure to walk along a soft turf path bordered with Scots pines. Keep straight on over a crosstrack. When you come to a gravel track turn right and follow this way quickly back to Churchplace. We are now on the track we followed at the beginning of our walk. When you reach the fourways again, turn right to make your way to the keeper's cottage. Through the gate, then left to see Ashurst Hospital and Lyndhurst Road Station a short distance ahead.

Notes for Walk 2

Note 1 *Churchplace*

The name suggests this could have been the site of a church of course, and if you explore the top you will find some interesting embankments. But was William such a villain as the Saxon chroniclers claim? According to the Winchester chronicle 'Through the space of thirty miles, the whole county, which was fruitful in a high degree, was laid waste. The churches, gardens, and houses were all destroyed, and the whole reduced by the king's order into a chase for beasts.' As many as thirty six parish churches are said to have been destroyed. Later historians question this. And that most warmhearted and outspoken of Hampshire travellers, William Cobbett, remarked as he rode through the Forest in 1823 that the area could never have been rich or populous — the soil was too poor. He pointed out that as in the original area of the Forest there still remain eleven parish churches on sites where churches were in existence before the time of the Conqueror, 'if he destroyed thirty six parish churches, what a populous county this must have been! There must have been forty seven parish churches over the whole district — one parish church to every four and three quarter square miles.' Have a look at this strange hill, and see what you think!

Note 2 *Cracknore*

Tales are told in 'It Happened in Hampshire' of smugglers who landed at Cracknore, loaded their contraband onto horses with shoes reversed and led them over this heath to a house near the present Beaulieu Road Station. When houses have been rebuilt, several 'hides' have been found, some even containing rotting casks. Ipley Manor, just south of the wood, was a known sanctuary for smugglers. As late as 1873 a smuggler was caught red-handed with his cargo off Cracknore.

Marchwood village, inland from Cracknore, was originally called 'Kingsland' and was part of William's royal hunting ground. In Domesday we are told that 'Alwin holds Marchwood of the king' and there is a tradition that William Rufus stayed at a hunting lodge near Bury Farm close by. Above Marchwood is one of the many beacon hills in Hampshire. A fire was to be lit here when the Armada was sighted to warn 'the rangers of Beaulieu'. In times past when every village had its quota of officials, "the Hayward" had to ensure that hedges were kept in repair. I am told there is still a Hayward at Marchwood. He has no salary, but is entitled to claim from owners of ponies which have been impounded for straying! Marchwood has also preserved its May Day verses.

May Day, or garland day, was a chance for the village children to glean a few pennies. The children tied flowers to the end of a stick, then, dressed in their best, went round the houses singing their May Day verse which ran:—

> A branch of May we have brought you,
> And at your door it stands.
> It's a very fine sprout,
> And well spread about,
> It's the work of our Lord's hands.

At Christmas, Marchwood, like so many villages, had its mummers. The mummers were bands of locals disguised in colourful costumes who went from house to house performing plays which involved a fine battle between St George and a Turkish Knight — the latter often abbreviated to Turkeysnipe!

The origin of these plays probably lies in the first simple acting by the congregation of scenes from the Bible in their churches. These had developed into plays by the beginning of the twelfth century, the earliest being the story of St Katherine dated about 1100. The resurrection was always a popular theme and the mummers' plays include a scene where the hero dies in combat with the villain and is then brought to life again. The Crusades have also left their mark in the frequent character of Saladin.

The Great Woods of Lyndhurst

This walk takes us through the marvellous woods of great oak and beech trees that surround the Forest capital, Lyndhurst. As we walk, I will describe some of the people you would once have met there making a living in these ancient woods. Today, of course, some Forest homes still retain their rights of common, entitling their occupants to graze their animals and gather fuel in the Forest. But not so long ago, the Forest was the home of the gypsies and other folk whose livelihoods welded them firmly to the area; for example adder catchers and CHARCOAL BURNERS (see Note 1). Many of the tracks we follow through these great woods were made by them.

The distance round is about six and a half miles and can be well accomplished in half a day. We start from Swan Green, a small hamlet close to Lyndhurst beside the A35 road to Bournemouth. The Bournemouth bus stops here or, as it is so close, you can walk from Lyndhurst. If you are coming by car from Southampton, turn right off the A35 at Swan Green, in the direction of Emery Down. After about a hundred yards turn into Swan Green car park on your left. Between the car park and the A35 is a wide green used as a cricket pitch. Our footpath climbs through the trees on the opposite side of the green from the car park from a point close to the main road. From the car park, walk diagonally downhill across the green towards the rails which border the A35, heading for the corner by the road where the rails meet the wooded slopes of Lyndhurst Hill. Just before you reach the rails you will see our path climbing steeply through the trees running roughly parallel with the main road.

29

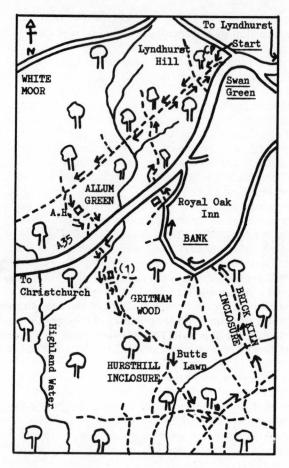

If you arrive at Swan Green by bus, walk beside the main road in the direction of Bournemouth for a few yards. Go through the gate at the edge of the green on your right to our path leading immediately uphill on the left. Follow this narrow woodland path as it climbs through oaks, beeches and hollies to the top of Lyndhurst Hill. The highest point is crowned by a magnificent stand of beeches. Then our route winds downhill beneath arches of spreading boughs with occasional glimpses of soft Forest lawns on either side. As I came down the hill a dainty roe deer skipped across my path to stand motionless in the shadow of the trees watching me pass. Cross two streams to more open heathland. On the left our path is now bordered by part of the walled garden of ALLUM HOUSE (see Note 2). The wall is beautifully built of warm red brick and our way follows its curve left round the building then right over Allum Green. Follow the track to the main road, the A35. Cross the cattle grid, turn right and walk beside the road for about a hundred yards. Look for a narrow path leading to a gate on the left. Cross the road, go through the gate and a wide green path leads you over a stream and into the oak and beech shaded glades of Gritnam wood. Ignore a track to the right and keep straight on for a short way until you see glimpses of cottages through the trees ahead. This is GRITNAM, (see Note 3) a compact Forest hamlet, completely encircled by these ancient woods. Bear a little right towards the cottages and follow the road round the hamlet, the houses on your left. Just past some white cottages our road round the village turns sharply left. Before this turn, directly in front of the cottages, take the green path that leads right into the heart of these glorious woods, towards Hursthill Inclosure. As I walked beneath magnificent oaks swathed to their upper boughs in holly and through groves of silver-grey beeches my feet crunched through thick layers of acorns and beech mast, or seed. This is still grazed today during the PANNAGE SEASON (see Note 4), but it was once the Forest's most valuable harvest. In the Domesday book, the worth of Forest holdings was assessed by the number of pigs their crop of mast could support. William Gilpin, vicar of Boldre, touring the Forest at the beginning of the nineteenth century, writes in great detail about the swineherd's task, particularly his slow and careful method of introducing the animals to the Forest (see Note 5).

C J Cornish, writing about the Forest in 1894, tells about

other people who made a living in these great woods, the charcoal burners. 'In a centre of a clearing', he writes, 'surrounded on three sides by a towering ring of monster beeches, was a deserted charcoal burner's hut, with a burning circle in front of the door. The hut looks like a large ant hill covered with scales of turf turned grass inwards, with a kind of mushroom cup on the apex and a square door and porch hewn of roughly squared oak. A glimpse of the interior shows that the framework is a cone of strong oak poles, and the only furniture a couple of sacks of dry beech leaves, a low wooden bench, and one or two iron pots'.

Cornish tells too of another, much stranger occupation. 'A similar hut' he writes, 'in Gritnam wood is inhabited throughout the year by an adder hunter. He lives in health and comfort with a low oak bench for his bed, and a faggot of heather for curtain and door.' Adder fat was much valued for medicinal purposes and adder hunting was a profitable business (see the Note on Brusher Mills, Walk 1).

Follow the path straight on through Gritnam wood to a fork. Here, bear right to leave the old trees and cross a grove of silver birches. Ahead you will see a gate with a stile beside it. Cross the stile into Hursthill Inclosure. Follow the track bearing left to join a gravel track. These are mixed woods; newly planted pines stand in the shadow of taller ones, rivalled still by the occasional oak and beech. Keep to the gravel track, crossing a wooden bridge over a stream. When you come to a T-junction turn left to walk the short distance to a gate leading out of the Inclosure. Through the gate turn left and follow the gravel track leading across an area known as Butts Lawn. 'Butts' as a placename occurs several times in the Forest. Possibly this name (meaning a target) dates from the days of archery when every English yeoman was compelled by law to practise shooting with the longbow. Only if a man practised from boyhood did his back muscles become sufficiently strong to bend the massive and deadly yew bows. Our gravel way curves round to the left to point us in a homeward direction. Go through the gate ahead into Brickkilns Inclosure. Now you are walking in new woods of slender saplings. In the past older trees were possibly used, as the name of the Inclosure suggests, to fire kilns to bake bricks. Until quite recent times, most villages had their own BRICKWORKS (see Note 6) which were used to rebuild cottages formerly constructed in the old mud walled manner.

Our track through Brickkilns Inclosure leads to a gate opening onto a minor road. The road runs from Lyndhurst — to the right of us — through the little village of Bank to meet the A35 at a point just south of Lyndhurst Hill. We aim to rejoin our earlier track at the foot of the Hill. From the gate leading out of Brickkilns Inclosure turn left and follow the road round until you can look over a huddle of red-roofed cottages to the shallow valley through which the A35 runs to Lyndhurst. Far right, on the hill top, rises the spire of Lyndhurst church and beyond the road ahead is the steep slope of Lyndhurst Hill. Walk down the road through the village, bearing right past a cottage dated 1600 and up the lane in front. When you come to the Royal Oak Inn on your left, turn right onto the road leading to the A35. Follow this lane for only a few yards — look carefully for a copse on the left. Beside the copse, a narrow path runs downhill to the road. Follow this path, copse on the right, to a gate by the A35. (If you miss this path, follow the lane to the main road, then turn left and walk the few yards to the gate.) Cross the main road, turn left, and a few yards further on you will see a gate into the Forest on your right. Go through the gate and ahead of you is a wide green lawn that appears to have no track across it. However, bear right along the edge of the woods for a few yards to pick up a good track running straight ahead across the lawn through the outlying trees of Lyndhurst Hill. Cross a narrow clearing with a concrete bridge over a stream, and follow the track straight into the woods ahead. Climb a few yards uphill to rejoin the path we followed at the beginning of our walk. Turn right and follow the path over Lyndhurst Hill and down to the corner beside the rails by the A35 at Swan Green. Lyndhurst is ahead and the car park lies diagonally across the green.

Notes for Walk 3

Note 1 *Charcoal Burners*

Charcoal burning was an important Forest industry. Charcoal was used to smelt iron until the use of coke became general and was an ingredient in the manufacture of gunpowder. A large gunpowder works flourished in the Forest at Eyeworth near Fritham until 1910. The making of charcoal was a slow and skilled occupation demanding the careful exclusion of air throughout the whole burning process so the men lived in the

Forest in wigwam shaped huts of branches and turf beside their 'hearths' where the wood was burnt. Mr Bill Veal of Emery Down recalls that his grandfather 'Old Marky' Veal used to supply charcoal for the use of Queen Victoria at Osborne House on the Isle of Wight. There was a temporary revival of the industry during the 1914-18 War.

Note 2 *Allum House*

Allum House is typical of the family homes built or acquired by wealthy business or professional men after the coming of the railway in the mid nineteenth century made the Forest more accessible. The Forest provided the seclusion and sporting facilities such homes required without the need of maintaining an estate. This pleasant house was once the home of the Fenwick family, who donated the hospital which bears their name to Lyndhurst in 1908.

Note 3 *Gritnam*

Gritnam has remained a perfectly compact Forest settlement without any tendency to straggle into the surrounding woods. Evidently the people who live there have always liked it that way for I came across a revealing story in 'It Happened in Hampshire'. An old cottager recalls her grandmother telling her that one day a queen (she wasn't certain which one) was riding past Gritnam and tore her dress. Her grandmother mended the tear and the queen gave permission for her family to take in from the Forest as much ground as they could dig within a certain specified time. No-one did any digging, the permission lapsed and Gritnam had no additions made to its boundaries!

Note 4 *The Pannage Season*

The pannage season when pigs may be turned out by the Commoners into the Forest begins in September, when the acorns and beech mast have fallen. Ponies nibble these also and, as too much is bad for them, the pigs perform a useful service as well as enjoying what must be the highlight of their year. The numbers of pigs you will see in the Forest are far fewer than in earlier days. William Cobbett, the fiery reformer, was delighted to see so many of these valuable animals — the mainstay of cottage economy — as he rode to Lyndhurst in

1820. He wrote 'of pigs this day we saw many, many thousand. I should think we saw at least a hundred hogs to one deer. I stopped at one time and counted the hogs and pigs just around me, and they amounted to one hundred and forty, all within fifty or sixty yards of my horse.'

Note 5 *Taming the Pigs*

Gilpin writes 'The method of treating hogs at this season of migration, and of reducing a large herd of these unmanageable brutes to perfect obedience and good government, is curious. The first step the swine-herd takes is to investigate some close sheltered part of the forest, where there is a conveniency of water; and plenty of oak, or beech mast . . . he fixes next on some spreading tree, round the bole of which he wattles a slight, circular fence . . . covering it roughly with boughs and sods, he fills it plentifully with straw or fern.' He then gets together his herd of five or six hundred pigs, then 'having driven them to their destined habitation, he gives them a plentiful supper of acorns or beech mast sounding his horn during the repast. He then turns them into the litter where, after a long journey and a hearty meal, they sleep deliciously.' The swine-herd watches them for three days then 'he leaves them a little more to themselves, having an eye however on their evening hours. But as their bellies are full, they seldom wander far from home, retiring commonly, very orderly to bed.' After this, he throws the sty open leaving his well-behaved animals to cater for themselves!

Note 6 *Local Brickworks*

To see local bricks used delightfully, visit Bucklers Hard beside the Beaulieu river. The brickworks still remain a short distance upstream towards Beaulieu and have been restored. The works provided labour for all. In 1893, a Chandlers Ford schoolmaster reported 'in Summer the boys are kept at work every minute they are out of school, and are constantly up all night burning bricks, so that they are ill-fitted for being taught next day.'

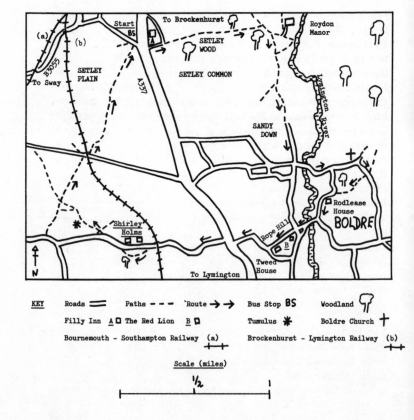

To Brockenhurst

Start
BS

SETLEY
WOOD

Roydon
Manor

(a)

(b)

B3055

SETLEY
PLAIN

To Sway

A337

SETLEY COMMON

Lymington River

SANDY
DOWN

Shirley
Holms

Rope Hill

Rodlease
House

BOLDRE

Tweed
House

To Lymington

N

KEY   Roads ══   Paths - - -   `Route → →   Bus Stop BS   Woodland

Filly Inn A □ The Red Lion B □   Tumulus ✳   Boldre Church ✝

Bournemouth - Southampton Railway (a)   Brockenhurst - Lymington Railway (b)

Scale (miles)

½   1

Exploring Boldre Village

It is easy to miss Boldre, a quiet, rather remote village, tucked away in the Forest beside the river a mile or two north of Lymington. But it is a fascinating place with a wealth of stories to add to our Forest lore. Among other delights you will find an ancient church where Robert Southey, better known as a Lake District writer, married his second wife, New Forest poetess Catherine Bowles. We pass a house used by smugglers, a school built by a local man in gratitude when the villagers rescued him from pirates, and find out why a special service is held every year in the church which draws people from many different parts of the British Isles. A great many of the houses around Boldre and in the village itself were built during the eighteenth century, restful and satisfying in their design. So you will find Boldre lovely to look at as well as interesting.

Our walk starts from close to the Filly Inn at Setley, a mile south of Brockenhurst on the A337 to Lymington. Driving from Brockenhurst, follow the Lymington road until you come to the Filly Inn on the left. Just past the Inn, you will see a minor road signposted to New Milton and Sway on your right. Turn into this road and you will find space to park beyond the bus stop. For those using public transport the bus service is number 56 running from Southampton via Brockenhurst to Lymington. Our route begins from the stop on the corner of the Sway road known as 'Setley New Inn'. The stop to catch the bus back to Brockenhurst is opposite. The walk is about six and a half miles round.

From the bus stop at the corner of the Sway road, cross the

A337 to a narrow lane marked with a No Through Road sign. Follow the lane as it dips downhill into Setley Wood. Go through the gate into the wood following the public bridle way. I was startled as I walked along the dry path by a large, coal black rabbit which appeared suddenly under the gorse bushes, looked at me for a moment then scampered off to join his more ordinary companions who took no notice of me at all! Our way runs through groves of silver birches and stands of enormous Scots pines. The pines, their flaking russet bark overlaid in patterns like wave marks on a beach, are some of the most beautiful I have seen. Among them stands the occasional solitary twisted shape of an ancient oak, survivors of former woods. When you come to a crossing bear right, past the lodge at the gates of Roydon Manor and keep straight on following the direction indicated by the footpath sign. The lane here is bordered by more ancient oaks, their branches contorted and embossed to such an extent that it is easy to imagine goblin faces among them and to understand why the Forest is so full of tales of Puck and his fellow hobgoblins, taking a mischievous delight in leading travellers astray. We find a wood called 'Puckpits', 'Puckmoor' and a burial mound, or barrow, on Beaulieu common which was once known as 'Pixey's cave'. I saw no goblins, only the inquisitive face of a squirrel glancing down at me with his shiny shoe-button eyes!

Our pleasant lane leads to a crossroads. Turn left for Boldre church. Before reaching the church we cross a bridge over the Boldre, or Lymington river. Here the river flows strongly through lush meadows dotted with dreamy-looking cattle. Willows trail in the water and below the bridge is a small island, golden with kingcups in the Spring and edged by long weed fronds waving snakily under the surface. Ducks quack busily about in the shallows to complete a perfect picture!

From the stream climb the lane to BOLDRE CHURCH (see Note 1) which overlooks the valley. This lovely old Forest church welcomes you with its homely weathered stone and comfortable-looking box pews. Allow some time to look round as it is full of interest. And now the twentieth century comes into our story. Boldre is known nationally as 'The Hood' church. Here you will find a memorial to HMS Hood. A commemoration service, attended by many relatives of the men who died in her, is held each year on a Sunday near to May 24, the date of her sinking.

From the church, follow the lane bearing right down to a bridge. A scattering of broken acorns on the coping showed where a squirrel had enjoyed a hearty breakfast! A few yards up the hill brings you to a footpath sign on the right. Follow this path through a wood fringed by a hazel coppice. As I came this way in early Spring each hazel bud was breaking into twin leaves which hung along the boughs still a little crumpled, resembling tiny green socks pegged out to dry! The path brings us down to a lane where we turn left for Boldre past Rodlease House. Smugglers used to 'borrow' the horses out of the stables at Rodlease at night and return them in the morning with their fee — a cask or two of good French brandy. Turn right at the next road junction to cross a fine five-arched stone bridge into Boldre.

As you walk up the hill through the village, past elegant eighteenth century houses, look for Boldre Lane, a small road on the left. Here you will find the village shop and post office. I was not surprised to be told that this charming low ceilinged building dated back to the beginning of the eighteenth century. I also heard that the neighbouring house with high pointed windows was originally a school. This was built before William Gilpin (see Note 1) endowed a later building and the story connected with it was a fascinating one. Evidently the owner of Tweed House (we shall be passing this large house shortly) was unlucky enough to be captured by pirates. The pirates demanded a ransom which the villagers paid, and in gratitude he built a school for their children when he returned. The story was told to me as if it all happened yesterday and somehow you feel very close to the past in Boldre.

Memories of the Civil War linger long in the Forest. Until recently, in Boldre, on oakapple day the children wore sprigs of oak. Non-wearers were greeted with cries of 'Sheet shacks', an old word for an oakapple.

Pass the half-timbered Red Lion Inn and climb Rope Hill. Tweed House is on the left of the road. The name 'Rope Hill' is a reminder of the days when rope making was a Forest industry. At the top of the hill we meet the A337 again. Cross the main road and turn left down the minor road leading to Shirley Holms; another intriguing name and as fascinating a place as the name suggests! Follow the road under the railway and you come to the Holms. 'Holms' are hollies and here is the most extraordinary oak wood — each tall tree is ringed by its attendant hollies which have grown long sinuous trunks as if they wished to imitate the oaks. So the hollies spread dark branches overhead, just beneath the level of the oak tree boughs. You walk beneath an evergreen canopy of sparkling holly leaves twisted as they are to point all ways to catch the light. To enjoy this experience, turn left off the minor road along a track into the wood opposite a black and white cottage. After a short distance you emerge onto an open hillside. Turn right and follow the track as it leads you back to the Shirley Holms road again. We have about a mile and a half of heathland to cross on our right to return to our starting point at Setley. When you rejoin the minor road, turn left and continue along it for a few yards until you come to a white path leading over the heath on the right. It is important to choose the right path here as there are several, so use the large mound you see ahead — a Bronze Age tumulus covered in gorse — as a guide. Pick up the track which passes just to the right of the mound. Follow the track another few yards to a fork. Turn right here, then at another crosspath right again along a green raised way leading towards the railway bridge over a minor road which you will see ahead. Turn right along the minor road, under the railway, and immediately on your left you will see a good track leading you over Setley Plain. Across the plain you will see the cream walls, black shutters and tall chimneys of the Filly Inn about half a mile distant. Keep straight ahead following a slightly raised path in the direction of the A337 and the Inn. It does not really matter which track you follow at this point — there are many — so long as you head for the main road. The green way brought me to the A337 a few yards from our destination, the bus stop at the corner of the Sway road. This walk is really a journey into time. I am sure you will enjoy it as much as I did!

Notes for Walk 4

Note 1 *Boldre Church*

The church of St John the Baptist at Boldre dates from the twelfth century, though there may well have been an earlier church on the site. Its distance from the village is probably due to its original purpose, to serve as a 'halfway house' for the monks travelling to Christchurch and Beaulieu. Traditionally, Boldre church door key was removed from Beaulieu Abbey at its dissolution in 1539. And now I *did* find strange faces looking down at me! These were the carved bosses in the roof of the nave, some of them very devilish in expression. There are traces of medieval wall paintings and in a glass case is a rare 'breeches' Bible — so called because in this edition it was considered more decorous for Adam and Eve to make themselves breeches out of fig leaves than the usual aprons. And here, in his own church, I found a portrait of Boldre's most famous vicar, William Gilpin. He was presented with the living in 1777 at a time when, it was said, his parishioners were notorious as little better than a set of bandits! Apart from writing his book on the 'picturesque' which made him famous, Gilpin worked hard for his parishioners, endowing a school and a poor house. In 1791 there is a fascinating entry in the church register. Two weddings were to be solemnised about the same time. When the customary registration tax of threepence was demanded, one of the bridegrooms objected; the other gallantly said he would pay for both of them, explaining that his wife would not be worth having if not considered worth an additional threepence. There is no record of what either wife said! Apart from Gilpin, Boldre church has more literary associations. Here, poet-laureate Robert Southey married his second wife, Caroline Bowles.

Boldre's special importance as the 'Hood' church gives this quiet building unique interest. HMS Hood was the flagship of Vice-Admiral L. E. Holland who lost his life in the tragedy. He had been a regular worshipper at Boldre and his widow arranged for the memorial to be placed in the church. This includes an illuminated book of remembrance containing the names of all those who lost their lives; and a painting of HMS Hood given by the eminent marine artist, Montague Dawson.

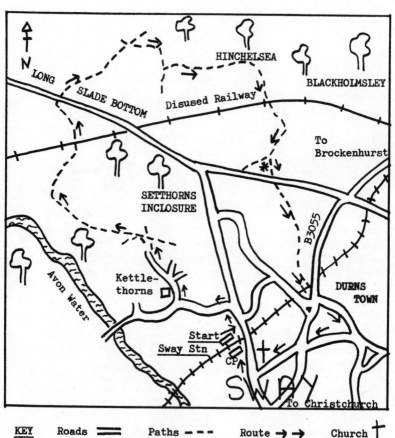

Something of a Mystery: Sway

At first glance there seems to be nothing mysterious about Sway but follow this walk to discover differently! Sway appears to be a quiet village to the south of the Forest in the area where Captain Marryat set his 'Children of the New Forest', a few miles north of Lymington. It lies each side of the Southampton to Bournemouth railway and is now just outside the official southern boundary of the Forest. It is however, still a true Forest village and, as you will find out, a place of fascinating mysteries!

The first puzzle I had to solve concerned Sway's exact position. Old maps show the village close to the little hamlet of Tiptoe so in the last hundred years Sway has moved a mile and a half west! The answer lies in the coming of a new railway (see Note 1).

Our walk, about five and a half miles round, starts from Sway station. Buses from Lymington stop here, and there is good parking close by. As we came out of the Station we noticed the date over the entrance — 1886 — too late for the original railway but right of course for the later one laid to Bournemouth. Turn right from the Station, then left, and walk through the village until you come to a fork. Our way is left here, down Mead End road. The other lane is called Brighton road, named after one of the gangs who came here to lay the railway. Another gang came from Manchester and gave their name to a road we pass on our return route. Walk a short way down Mead End road, then turn right down Adlams Lane which leads to SETTHORNS INCLOSURE (see Note 2). On the corner you pass a tall, old house with the enchanting name of KETTLETHORNS (see Note 3). It is a lovely lane, bordered by oaks, and dipping down to a footpath. Soon you come to a gate opposite Setthorns Inclosure. Go through the gate, cross the green lawn ahead, and through another gate into the wood. We had just closed the gate when a troupe of fallow deer with their distinctive white rumps ran across our path, heads held high, causing the faintest of rustling among the dead bracken as they disappeared among the oak trees. Our way heads west through Setthorns Inclosure then curves right to bring us out of the wood and over the old railway track at Setthorns cottage. Ignore the first left turn but when the path divides, bear left here. Traditional oaks and holly border the left side of our track, the other side is fringed by tall larches inter-planted with young pines. Now keep to this main track, straight over all crossways. Setthorns is a maze of paths rambling up and down hill. If you cannot resist some of these tempting ways, you could ramble round the Inclosure and return to Sway by one of several routes which a glance at the map would suggest.

Our wide way curves round to the right to lead through part of the wood that has recently been felled. This planting and harvesting of quick growing timber is vital if the Forest is to 'pay its way' in the twentieth century. But the FORESTRY COMMISSION (see Note 4) ensures that the beauty of the Forest is maintained — unlike earlier days.

Follow the path through the edge of the woods, past a camp site to a cattle grid. Turn left over the bridge across the track of the old railway then climb uphill to leave the Inclosure and join a minor road. Setthorns cottage is on your left. Turn left and follow the road for a few yards until you see a car park on your right. Cross the road and walk straight over the car park. Now you overlook a beautiful green expanse of turf, cropped short by the Forest ponies, called LONGSLADE BOTTOM (see Note 5). A 'slade' in the Forest means a little valley between wooded hills, which is just what you see.

We intend making for the left hand corner of the wood you see on the other side of Longslade; Hinchelsea wood. Over the green you will see our track clearly winding up the hillside towards the corner of the wood, the right hand of two paths. Cross the green to pick up the path and follow it uphill through the heath and gorse to the edge of Hinchelsea wood, which is fringed by stands of tall Scots pines. Go over a cross-track to the pines then turn right and walk east through the edge of this old wood. Half-hidden among the pines and undergrowth you will see remnants of ancient oaks, some only shells, survivors of the woods Gilpin regretted. Oak trees have always been specially vulnerable. Apart from their value as naval timber, their bark was used in tanning leather, a process known as 'rhining'. Sway was the centre of this Forest Industry. The rhine was dried until it was brittle and a piece of rhine 'as big as a penny was worth a penny'.

Walk along the edge of Hinchelsea wood for about half a mile until you come to a track leading steeply downhill on your right. This runs to the old railway again. Follow the path down and now we see some of the Forest's real wet lands. Our path is raised to cross shallow brooks widening into ponds full of tall waving sedge grasses. At one point an island of rhododendron bushes appears crowned by two minute pine trees. As I walked past I heard the harsh croak of a heron from deep within the reeds. Follow the track under the old railway and up the heath opposite to the minor road again. Before the road you pass another Bronze Age tumulus on the right of the path. Its soft green turf and sheltering gorse bushes make it an ideal place for a rest. From the tumulus look across the road and over the heath beyond to see a tall slim tower on the horizon beyond Sway. We are going to use this outstanding landmark to help us get our bearings right on the way back. It is known as SWAY TOWER (see Note 6) or Peterson's folly and may well qualify as another of Sway's puzzles! It was built between 1879 and 1884 by Andrew Thomas Turton Peterson, formerly a Judge of the High Court of Calcutta. One of the first buildings ever to be constructed of concrete, it was built without steel reinforcement by unskilled labour, 220 feet high with twelve rooms sixteen feet square one over the other, reached by a spiral staircase at the side.

Keeping your eyes on that tower, leaving the tumulus on your right, cross the minor road. The route now runs across the heath on the right in the direction of the tower. There are several paths so use the tower as your guide. Our aim is to cross the railway and walk back to the Station through the Durns Town area of Sway. Follow the track across the heath towards the tower, ignoring all side tracks. The long gentle curving line of the Isle of Wight downs forms the horizon ahead of us. Cross the railway bridge and walk over the common to a cattle grid over the B3055. Turn right along this road through Durns Town. This is the oldest part of Sway and you will see several traditional Forest cottages. Durns Town may have derived its name from the family called Durrant who farmed here in the seventeenth and eighteenth centuries. Before that, in the Forest perambulation of 1670, it was called the hamlet of Stamford after the brook that now flows under the road at the foot of Back Lane. You will see Back Lane on the left, just before you come to a crossroads. At the crossroads turn right down Church Lane. As you might expect, you pass Sway church, a pleasant early Victorian church built in the Gothic style. The church was built in 1838 when life in Sway had much more in common with the England of the first Queen Elizabeth! Bishop Sumner, arriving to consecrate the church a year later, came on horseback. Some ladies who were decorating the church told me, among many other stories about Sway which I have included in this chapter, that old residents could remember horse drawn cabs driving through the Forest to collect visitors from London. You can hire horse drawn buggies today in various parts of the Forest, so we may be able to recapture some of the charm of these peaceful days!

Inside the church, I found more of Sway's mysteries. The church is dedicated to St Luke but on the foundation stone we read 'dedicated to St Mark'. What can we make of that? On the window sill in the north wall of the Sanctuary is an urn containing the ashes of an Egyptian christian who lived two hundred years after Christ. How did this find its way to St Luke's? On the north wall is an ancient crucifix found near Sway some years ago. How old? Who found it and where? Nobody appears to have the definite answers.

At the end of Church Lane turn right and you will see the Station ahead. Before you leave Sway, I must add what a charming little Victorian station this is. It was the winner of the best kept station award in the Bournemouth area in 1976. You don't often see waiting rooms decorated with cacti and pot plants, do you? But anything is possible at Sway — there is a definite air of magic about the whole place!

Notes for Walk 5

Note 1 *Tiptoe or Sway?*
I discovered that Tiptoe was the original area of Sway, a much

smaller place than today's village. During Victorian days the boom in seaside development turned the sleepy hamlet of Bourne into the flourishing resort of Bournemouth. People wanted seaside holidays and the existing railway, laid in the mid-nineteenth century was of little use to them. It ran from Southampton to a point about a mile south of Brockenhurst, then west across the Forest through Wimborne Minster to Poole. So a new line was laid from just south of Brockenhurst to take them to Bournemouth. At the same time inclosures were made in the Sway area. So Sway moved to its present position as a home both for the railway workers and the folk engaged in forestry. The result of this mixture of old and new gives Sway a special attraction; you will find that ancient cob-walled cottages blend happily here with Victorian brick.

Note 2 *Setthorns*
William Gilpin rode through Setthorns at the end of the eighteenth century. (His parish at Boldre included Sway). He comments sadly that once Setthorns 'was the noblest of all Forest scenes, the number of its oaks were the admiration of all who saw them. But its glories are now over. During the unremitted course of thirty years it continued to add strength to the fleets of Britain; itself sufficient to raise a Navy. In this arduous service its vigour was at length exhausted; and it contains little more at present than shrubs and underweed ...'. Today we are more fortunate. The mighty oaks may have gone, but with the careful replanting of Setthorns we can enjoy some of its former glory.

Note 3 *Kettlethorns*
'It Happened in Hampshire' tells us that a secret passage used by smugglers connects Kettlethorns with the sea. Another passage, four miles long, connected Sway House with the coast. South of Sway, leading off Silver Street, is Agars Lane, so frequently used by smugglers that it is said that the deep ruts formed by their waggon wheels may still be traced! Presumably the smugglers would lead their ponies down Adlams Lane to cross the Forest.

Note 4 *The Forestry Commission*
The work of the Commission who administer the Forest is extremely varied. Under their care, the Forest is replanted so

47

that the old woods — the 'ancient and ornamental woodlands' are preserved and at the same time softwoods are planted and harvested to make sure the Forest is economically viable as well as beautiful. The Commission works closely with the New Forest Consultation Panel who represent all who have interests in the Forest. They include the Commoners who need land cleared and drained for their animals, conservationists, residents, campers, and walkers.

Note 5 *Longslade Bottom*

This is how Gilpin describes our view, nearly two hundred years ago. You will find it has changed very little! 'A beautiful valley, about a quarter of a mile in breadth, opened before us, arrayed in vivid green, and winding two or three miles round a wood. On the other side the grounds, wild and unadorned, fall with an easy sweep into it. Beyond these a grand woody scene spreads far and wide into the distance ... the valley was no other than that vast bog, Longslade Bottom. The nimble deer trips over it in summer without inconvenience, but no animals of heavier bulk dare trust themselves upon it ...' But there is no need to worry about crossing it today. One change that has occurred is an improvement in drainage!

Note 6 *Sway Tower*

The Forest saying goes that there are as many steps in the tower as there are days in the year and as many windows as there are weeks! Mr Peterson wanted to put a light at the top, but was forbidden by the Board of Trade who suspected it would confuse shipping. But what could have led the retired judge to build such a home? Various stories circulate — one is that His Honour intended to be buried at the top and his wife at the bottom, thus showing his superiority! If this were true, he was disappointed; Mrs Peterson was buried in Sway churchyard and Mr Peterson's ashes at the foot of his tower. In 1957 they were transfered to his wife's grave. Another story claims that Mr Peterson, being an ardent Spiritualist, received communications through a medium from Sir Christopher Wren. The great architect gave his pupil directions for mixing the concrete and pointed out to him errors in laying his foundations.

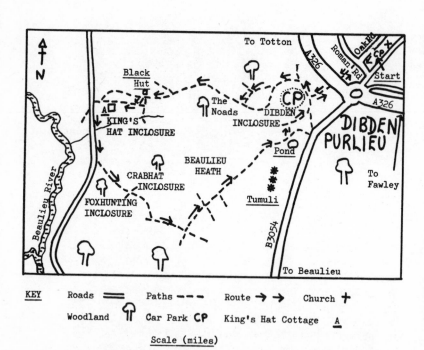

KEY	Roads ═══	Paths ‑ ‑ ‑	Route →→	Church ✝
	Woodland 🌳	Car Park **CP**	King's Hat Cottage **A**	

Scale (miles)

Of Hats and Noads and Roman Roads: Dibden Purlieu

This short ramble will provide you with the most delightful kind of potted history of the Forest. We begin on the Roman Road mentioned in the title, then go on to discover the noads, a Forest term for burial mounds raised in the Bronze Age, some three thousand years ago. You will find 'hats' dotted about all over the Forest! (See note 1). This is not the result of unusually high winds but just another curious local name. Any eminent group of trees, perhaps strikingly tall or on a hill, is called a 'hat'. Sometimes the name remains after the original trees have been felled. We shall be walking through 'Kings Hat' and 'Crab Hat'.

The walk is about four miles round — perfect on a clear afternoon. There are splendid views and every variety of Forest scenery, oak woods, heathland, and green lawns. Our starting place is DIBDEN PURLIEU (see Note 2) which is about two and a half miles south west of Hythe on the eastern boundary of the Forest. Driving from Totton, take the A326 which bypasses Marchwood and Dibden. After the turning to Dibden you approach a roundabout. Turn left here for Dibden Purlieu, then immediately left again into Roman Road which runs parallel with the A326 at this point. A short way down Roman Road you will see a free car park sign pointing down Oak Road on your right. Follow the sign to the car park on the right, behind a new church. From the car park, turn left and walk back up Oak Road to ROMAN ROAD (see Note 3). Across the road you will see a track with a seat beside it. The track leads over the grass verge to cross the A326 to a gate into Dibden

Inclosure where we begin our walk. If you come to Dibden Purlieu by bus from Hythe or Lymington, get off at the Heath Hotel by the roundabout. Cross the road leading to Dibden Purlieu and you will see Roman Road a little to your right. Walk down Roman Road to the free car park sign and on the left you will see the track by the seat.

Follow the track over the grass verge. Cross the A326 and take the path straight ahead which leads to a stile, the sort you have to squeeze through, a speciality of this part of the Forest! Before you stretches a green lawn, backed by the trees of Dibden Inclosure. This is one of several man-made lawns in the Forest. These areas were seeded by the Forestry Commission by agreement with the commoners when new inclosures were made along this eastern boundary in 1959. Go through another stile and down the path into the inclosure through low growing gorse and willows and young pines, interplanted with beech saplings. When you come to a car park, follow the path right round part of it, then left down a wide, grassy way. The young pines stand close like a green wall behind tall mounds of heather. At the end of this wide walk you come to a gate and — as happens so often in the Forest — you go through it into a different world! First a fringe of birches, their leaves and silver bark shimmering in the sunlight, then shadowy glades beneath the bent and hoary shapes of old oaks encircled by their hollies. Under the oaks, the sunlight splashes the lawns and grasses and brightens the red of last years bracken, but among them stand enormous yews, darker than the hollies and under which nothing grows. But of all trees, the yew was once the most valued — and the most useful — perhaps that is why we see so few of them, except in churchyards. Their branches provided the pliant but powerful wood needed for the famous English LONG BOW (see Note 4). Look for yews in these old woods, especially by pathways as they were often planted as marker trees.

Keep straight on into the wood to a fork. Bear left here and soon you come out of the trees onto a more open area of heathland. It is quite narrow and another old wood faces you on the other side. Follow the path towards the second wood, but just before you reach it, you will find the path bears right. Now you are standing with the wood on your left, on the highest point of the heath, with a wonderful view westwards over the Forest. You look down on the great woods around the upper reaches of the Beaulieu river, then on to a dense wall of woodland around Lyndhurst and beyond the Forest to a line of hills on the horizon, the chalklands of Dorset. Our path leads us down the hillside and across a heath towards the right hand corner of a dark line of pines which form the edge of Kings Hat Inclosure. As you approach the pines, look for a gate leading into the Inclosure, a little to your left. Go through the gate and take the track ahead into these pinewoods. After the oakwoods, so full of life, it is very still beneath the pines, the scented air hardly moves beneath the dense canopy of their boughs. Today, we are so used to pine trees that it seems almost unbelievable that, apart from the Scots pine and the yew, they are relative newcomers to our islands, planted in the New Forest as an experiment in 1776. As they became more widespread as a profitable quick growing tree, some people objected. This story is told by that delightful countryside writer, Richard Jefferie. On one occasion, when visiting the Forest, he talked with a woodman's wife, whose lovely cottage lay away from the road surrounded by pine woods. He expressed his pleasure in her beautiful surroundings. 'I've had enough of it', was her reply, 'eighteen years; tis desprit lonesome. Past them ugly trees is the road, but you'll surely lose your way comin' back if you don't mark crosses with your sticks as ye go.' The Kings Hat pines are surely not as depressing as that! Look for one group of really outstanding young pines, a vivid shade of emerald green. Keep straight ahead, over all cross-tracks until you come to a small black hut on your right. Opposite, a yew tree indicates our way. (Ignore the more obvious gravel track which turns sharp left.) Take the green way which bears a little left, then right past a cottage you will glimpse through the trees on your left. Our way now brings us to a gate leading to a minor road. Go through the gate out of Kings Hat Inclosure and turn left to walk along the side of the road for about a quarter of a mile. Our path leads left over the heath just after the end of Kings Hat Inclosure fence. Turn left along this wide green way as it takes you over the open moor and then between the trees of Crabhat Inclosure on your left and those of Foxhunting Inclosure on your right.

Our way now lies through mixed woodlands of oaks, birches, sweet chestnuts and newly planted pines. Keep straight ahead, across a stream where the ground, being low-lying and wet is reddened with bushes of bog-myrtle, then up the slope opposite, following the path as it bears left to bring us onto the heath. We are now turning towards Dibden Purlieu, to make our way back across the eastern part of Beaulieu Heath. As you climb a shallow valley runs beside you on the left. Then the heath widens into a large expanse of flat moorland that so delighted W H Hudson. In his 'Hampshire Days' he writes of Beaulieu Heath: 'woods have a less enduring hold on the spirit than the open heath . . . it seems enough that it is open where the wind blows free, and there is nothing between us and the sun.' Contrast this with William Cobbett's view as he crossed Beaulieu Heath: 'A poorer spot than this New Forest there is not in all England', he grumbled, 'it's more barren and miserable than Bagshot Heath.' Of course, Cobbett was concerned about growing profitable crops, not watching wildlife.— everything depends upon your point of view!

Follow the track over the heath until you meet a path joining on the right. Turn left, then when the path forks, left again so that you are now facing Dibden Purlieu and walking in the direction of the B3054. As you walk back you will see all the different types of woodlands we have walked through neatly arranged beside you — the new pines of Dibden, the graceful varied outlines of the oak woods and the denser darker masses of the more mature pines. Close to the path on your right you will see three large barrows, or burial mounds. There are a hundred and seventy of these dotted all over the Forest. Constructed by the early Bronze Age people they are a reminder that men lived here over seventeen hundred years before the birth of Christ. Locally, they are known as the Noads.

Before you reach the B3054 you will see a small pond on your right, and on your left an opening in the Inclosure fence. Turn left here along the path leading into Dibden Inclosure. When you come to a crossways, turn right for just a few steps and you will see our path running left again. Follow this to a wide green way. Now we have rejoined our original path. Turn right and follow it round the car park, then through the gorse bushes on the left, over the lawn and back to the A326. Cross the main road and walk down Oak Road to the car park, or turn left down Roman Road for the bus stop.

Notes for Walk 6

Note 1 *'Hats'*

The historian, Heywood Sumner lists twenty-two 'hats' in the

Forest. They have charmingly descriptive names and include Great Dark Hat and Little Dark Hat, Great Stubby Hat and Little Stubby Hat, Ashen's Hat, Black Bush Hat, and the much more impressive Cardinal's Hat. John Wise suggests the word may have had its origin in the high-crowned hats worn by the Puritans in the time of Charles I.

The Forest has a way with words. For example in low lying areas fords are called 'passages', around Lyndhurst streams are called 'waters', and a little further north they become 'gutters'. The streams that flow south west into the Avon in the far north of the Forest are much more recognisable, they are called 'brooks'.

Note 2 *Dibden Purlieu*
The name is interesting, reflecting the people of the Forest and their livelihood. 'Dibden' is Saxon meaning a deep wooded valley. 'Purlieu' is from Norman-French; *Pur* -exempt, *Lieu* - place. This was land on the edge of the Forest that at some time in the past had been wrongfully included within the Forest perambulation, or official boundaries. Subsequently the error had been corrected and the land disafforested; it became no longer subject to the Forest Laws and could be farmed.

Note 3 *Roman Road*
This old road, possibly on the track of an earlier Celtic or Iron Age route, runs for part of its length beside the new Totton to Fawley road. Although its authenticity as a Roman road has been questioned, most authorities, including Margery, agree that it is genuine, connecting the important Forest port of Lepe (now decayed) with Southampton and Winchester in one direction, and Ringwood and the west in the other. In Roman times, and earlier, tin was brought from Cornwall down this road to be shipped from Lepe to the Isle of Wight and from there to France. Large masses of tin have been found close to the road.

Note 4 *The Long Bow*
The tall English long bow was quicker and more powerful than the crossbow. But shooting it required all a man's strength. Gilpin explains how the English archer 'did not, as in other nations, keep his left hand steady, and draw his bow with his right; but keeping his right at rest upon the nerve, he pressed the

whole weight of his body into the horns of the bow. Hence probably arose the English phrase of bending a bow; and the French of drawing one'. This irresistibly calls to mind Sir Arthur Conan Doyle's 'The White Company' part of which is set in this area of the Forest, and the 'Song of the Bow'. He was thinking of these yews when he wrote:

'Of true wood, of yew wood,
The wood of English bows.
So men who are free
Love the old yew tree
And the land where the yew tree grows ...'

Conan Doyle lived for a time in the Forest, at Bignal Wood, near Minstead. He is buried in Minstead churchyard.

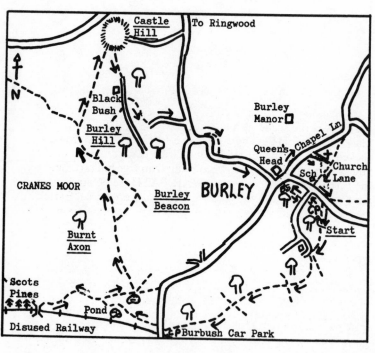

Castle Hill

To Ringwood

Black Bush

Burley Hill

Burley Manor

Chapel Ln

Queen's Head

Church Lane

Sch

CRANES MOOR

Burley Beacon

BURLEY

BS

CP

Start

Burnt Axon

Scots Pines

Pond

Burbush Car Park

Disused Railway

N

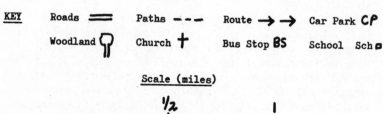

KEY   Roads ═══   Paths ‑ ‑ ‑   Route →→   Car Park CP

Woodland ♀   Church †   Bus Stop BS   School Sch ▪

Scale (miles)

½   1
├──────────────────────┤

Dragons, Smugglers and Battles Long Ago: Burley Moor

Can you imagine our peaceful Forest as a battleground? In the past it was the scene of many conflicts and the most exciting place to go to find out about them is Burley, an attractive village tucked away in the Forest's south west corner. South of the village runs a high ridge crowned by an Iron Age hill fort. Below the fort a Saxon *here-path* or WAR PATH (see Note 1) runs west to Ringwood in the Avon valley. The very name 'Burley' means 'a fortified place in a clearing'. It was a favourite haunt of smugglers whose road we follow over the moor. And close by, on Beacon Hill, surely the most amazing fight of all took place when brave Sir Moris tackled the local dragon!

I have planned this route to explore the scene of all these events. It is about five and a half miles round but as it involves a little gentle climbing and some wonderful viewpoints, allow a good half day, a whole day if you can. Burley, like Lyndhurst is well known for its cream teas and it would be a pity to rush away from so good an Inn as the Queen's Head where we begin and end our walk.

The Queen's Head stands at the junction of four roads at the head of Burley's main street. The bus from Southampton stops here. If you come by car I would advise leaving it in the large car park just before you enter the village. From Lyndhurst, follow the A35 (Bournemouth) road and turn right for Burley at Holmsley old Station. Drive past the golf course and you will see the car park I mean on your left. You can then walk the few yards down the road to the Queen's Head or follow the footpath leading from the car park. Go past a Forestry Commission barrier leaving a sign to 'Brenchley' on your left. Follow the path through the oaks and beeches downhill to the road facing the Queen's Head. The Queen's Head is a fascinating Inn, dating back to before 1650 and packed with treasures from the past including reminders of smuggling days, collections of old weapons, and relics of Forest life in former times.

Standing with the Inn on your left you will see a minor road straight ahead called Chapel Lane with a signpost to the Church. Follow this road for a few yards until you see a path, Church Lane, leading up the hillside on your right. Turn right and climb the short distance to the little Victorian church shaded by enormous yews and dedicated to St John the Baptist. It is probable there was a place of worship in Burley before 1550 as a deed of 1663 mentions a 'tenement called the chapel' and a field called Chapel Haye. This may have been a Chapel belonging to the Manor, which after the Reformation was left derelict to be used as a cottage. Burley was originally part of the parish of Ringwood and was only separated in 1838 when Sir John Lefevre, Lord of the Manor of Burley, gave part of his estate called Barn Close for the first Anglican church. A small Dames school was set up in the churchyard.

From the church gate you have a fine view of BURLEY MANOR (see Note 2) in the valley, surrounded by parkland. Although the name Burley is not in the Domesday Book, the Manor was probably laid out in Saxon times and must have existed then as no further extensive grants of land would have been made once William the Conqueror had decided to enclose the Forest.

Turn right from the church gate and follow the path ahead through the trees. You come out of the wood and pass the school on the right. Cross the minor road to the car park. Walk diagonally over the car park bearing left. Beyond a car free area barrier you will see our path, a white track leading south over the heath. Follow this straight ahead over all cross tracks. If you walk through the heather and gorse and small self-sown birches at the right time of year the scent from the fully opened flowers of the furze will rise through the warm air reminiscent of freshly grated coconuts. This heath above Goatspen Plain has a character all its own. The path dips and rises over shallow valleys and miniature hills presenting unexpected glimpses of a hidden Forest lawn, a half-concealed stream or a lonely wood.

Soon you come to a deeper valley with a white cottage beside an old barn standing to the right of our path. Turn left in front of the cottage and follow the track for a short distance along the valley. Then keep to the track as it bears right uphill and over the heath again. Across the heath on the right you will see the line of the old oak woods south of Burley. Follow the main track as it narrows through high gorse bushes and dips downhill. Our way bears a little right to bring us to a minor road that runs from Burley due south to Thorney Hill at the point where the road crosses the track of the old railway. To meet the road, you walk through Burbush car park. The railway bridge is on your left. Keeping the cutting through which the old railway runs on your left, cross the road and follow the path immediately ahead, running west, almost parallel with the railway. (This good path is not on the map but we shall soon join a path clearly marked.) You pass a small Forest pool. The path leads straight to the fringe of a little wood. Here another track (on the map) joins our way from the right. We shall be retracing our steps to this point later to follow this path, but the wood ahead is so lovely I would like you to see it first! Follow the path through some beautiful, very tall Scots pines to another bridge over the railway. Pause here among these silent pine groves to absorb their scent and colour; their rich red bark contrasting with their dark glossy leaves.

Retrace your path, bearing left at the fork until you come to a point where you have the choice of three paths. Follow the path furthest left, heading north across Cranes Moor. A long ridge formed by Burley Beacon, Burley Hill and Castle Hill runs beside you over the heath to your right. The whole area feels like an old battlefield and as John Wise, the Forest historian, tells us place names seem to prove it. We find 'Greater' and 'Lesser Castle Fields' and 'Barrows' and 'Coffins'. On Cranes Moor you will see strange shaped hummocks, a tumulus or ancient burial mound, and a curious wood of twisted oaks and thorns marked significantly on the map as 'Burnt Axon'. No doubt they were battle axes! Over to the right, Burley Beacon frowns down on us. Here signal fires were lit in times of danger and here, evidently, be dragons! There is a document in Berkeley Castle, of uncertain date, which tells the story of a fight between Sir Moris Barkley and 'A DEVOURING DRAGON' (see Note 3).

Follow the track over Cranes Moor, past the foot of Burley

Hill. This is one of several smugglers tracks leading from Thorney Hill, over Cranes Moor then north to Picket Post (now beside the A31) where there is said to be a bricked up cellar in which smuggled goods were stored. The path forks, one way leads to the minor road you will see directly ahead, but our way bears right up the hill to the corner of the oak wood crowning our destination, CASTLE HILL (see Note 4). The slope is rather steep, but you will find, as with most Forest hills, you are soon at the top. As you climb higher you will cross ditches and embankments and if you look back you will see the two loaf shaped hillocks guarding the approaches to this ancient hill fort. I sat on the ridges formed by the roots of some dwarf oak trees on the summit to enjoy one of the most wonderful views in the whole Forest area. Below you, rolling fields spread in soft waves over the Avon valley to mist — blue hills merging into the sky. A little to the right a break in the outline of the heath gives a glimpse of the Wiltshire Downs and to the left you will see the tower of Christchurch Priory. Close by our hill runs a minor road from Burley through Crow to Ringwood, this is the Saxon warpath I mentioned earlier.

Our return route is shorter as a good path runs from Castle Hill south along the top of the ridge past Black Bush, to Burley village. Follow this path along the ridge. Just past Black Bush cottage look for a footpath sign and a stile on your left. Cross the stile and follow the woodland path to meet a minor road. Turn left to leave the wood, following the footpath sign. The minor road brings you down to the busy road leading from Burley to Picket Post. Turn right and walk a few yards along the pavement, then follow the footpath sign leading you to a safe and very pleasant path to Burley village.

Burley was once so remote a Forest village that it was said to depend for its livelihood on its yearly crop of acorns and beech mast, or 'akermast' to use the local name. Not so today. This attractive village has many visitors. Souvenir shops display local crafts, paintings on velvet, and oil paintings. Some of the houses are very old, half-timbered, with their original open fireplaces. As you walk up the street towards the Queens Head you pass a paper shop with a square building beside it. This was the village smithy. The building's central position, near the top of the main street indicates how important the Smith was in former days. As well as shoeing horses, he made iron tyres for carts and mended tools. At the top of the street stands the Cross and facing it, behind a modern shop front is the building which a hundred years ago was the sole village shop, selling everything from bread and bacon to oil for the lamps and blacking for the kitchen grates. To the left of the Cross, you will see the Queens Head with the footpath to the car park opposite.

Notes for Walk 7

Note 1 *Saxon here-path or war path*
This road has been identified as a Saxon here-path by John Wise and Heywood Sumner, both noted Forest historians. 'Here' was the Saxon word for an army. According to the Anglo-Saxon chronicle the New Forest was the scene of a major invasion by Saxon tribes under their leaders Cerdic and Cynric in AD495. They landed at 'Cerdices ora' possibly Totton or Calshot, and advanced through the Forest to defeat the British at 'Natanleay', today called Netley Marsh. The name commemorates the British leader, Natan -leod. The area took some time to subdue for it was not until AD519 that the Saxons inflicted a conclusive defeat on the Britons close to the Avon at 'Cerdices ford', today's Charford, not far from Burley.

Note 2 *Burley Manor*
The manor certainly existed in Norman times and was owned by the de Burley family for two hundred years until it was ceded to the King in 1388 when Sir Simon de Burley was executed in the Tower of London for alleged treason. Sir Simon was tutor to the Black Prince. For the following two hundred years Burley was a Royal Manor but in 1550 a Tudor House was built here owned by the Batten family. This was replaced by a Georgian house, burnt down in 1850. After the fire, Colonel Esdaile had the central part of the house rebuilt in Tudor style. The manor was requisitioned by the Army during the last war, the lake was drained and many fine trees cut down. One remains — a cedar, possibly about a hundred and fifty years old on the south lawn. Now the manor is a hotel.

Note 3 *Burley Dragon*
The document reads: 'Sir Moris Barkley the son of Sir John Barkley, of Beverston, being a man of great strength and courage, in his time there was bred in Hampshire near Bisterne a devouring dragon, who doing much mischief upon men and

cattel and could not be destroyed but spoiled many in attempting it, making his den near unto a Beacon. This Sir Moris Barkley armed himself and encountered with it and at length overcame and killed it but died himself soon after.' There are two Dragon Fields near Bisterne and the Green Dragon Inn at Brook probably is also a reminder of this legend for the redoubtable Sir Moris was also Lord of the Manor of Minstead and Brook. I saw no dragons but even today the area looks wild and remote enough to be the home of one!

Note 4 *Castle Hill*

A 'Castle' in the Forest means an Iron Age or pre-Roman fort or protected settlement. Today the encircling ditches and embankments remain, often enclosing a large area where the first settlement could be made and where later the whole village could gather with their animals for safety. Originally the embankments would have been crowned by high timber pallisades with massive gates. Dating back to about 500 BC, they indicate that the population of the Forest was fairly sparse. No Forest fort is comparable in size with those in Dorset.

Historians can tell us little about the part played by the Forest forts during the early days of the Roman invasion. Sufficient remains however to indicate that strategically the Forest was important as it lay directly in the path of the Roman advance towards Dorset. Later the area seems to have settled down peacefully under Roman rule. Pottery was made locally and at Sloden near Dockens Water, which was exported to different parts of the Empire.

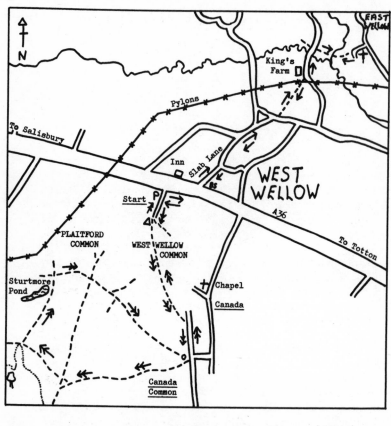

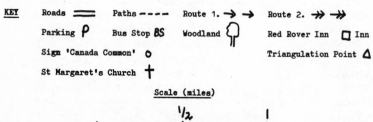

KEY

Roads ═══	Paths - - - -	Route 1. → →	Route 2. ⇉ ⇉
Parking ℗	Bus Stop **BS**	Woodland 🌳	Red Rover Inn ☐ Inn
Sign 'Canada Common' ○			Triangulation Point △
St Margaret's Church ✝			

Scale (miles)

½   1

Between Two Worlds:
West Wellow

The northern boundary of the Forest has a special fascination because when the extent of the Forest was defined there was no natural feature that made an obvious limit. To the west lay the Avon, to the east Southampton Water and to the south the Solent; only in the north was there any real difficulty. The people living there clung firmly to their 'Commons', the land each village shared in common adjoining the Forest. But this led to problems. Could they kill the King's deer if one crossed the boundary? And what happened to their own animals if they strayed illegally into the Forest? These villages found themselves quite literally between two worlds! I have planned two walks in this chapter, both starting from the same place: West Wellow.

One of them, about three and a half miles round, explores two of these Commons and takes you along the northern boundary of the Forest. The other walk, about three miles round, also illustrates the idea of existing between two worlds, but in a very different way. It is a kind of pilgrimage, in the steps of one of the world's greatest heroines, Florence Nightingale, who lived at Embley Park, close to East Wellow. Born a Victorian lady, in her struggle against prejudice and disease she was a pioneer of much we can be proud of in our modern world. We walk through lovely countryside to East Wellow, to the tiny church where she worshipped and is buried. The church contains many fascinating mementos of her including one of the field lamps she carried at Scutari.

As both these walks are so short you can do them consecutively if you wish. Allow time to look round the church at East Wellow and up to three hours for the longer walk. It includes a beautiful stretch of water where you may see herons and other interesting wildlife. Both walks start from THE RED ROVER INN (see Note 1) at West Wellow. West Wellow lies beside the main road from Southampton to Salisbury, the A36. If you are driving from Southampton, go through the village to pass the Red Rover on your right. A few yards further you will see a gravel track leading to a cattle grid on your left. Turn in here, cross the grid, and you will find room to park beside the track.

For the shorter walk to East Wellow, walk back past the Red Rover and down the hill towards the bus shelter. Before the shelter, a minor road, Slab Lane, leads into the village on your left. This is our way. If you arrive on the bus — there is a good service from Southampton via Totton — cross the A36 and Slab Lane is on your right.

Walk up Slab Lane, passing the intriguingly named Gazing Lane on your right. The Wellows delight in such thought provoking names! You will also find 'Monkey's Jump' and 'Boxing Corner'. Soon you will see a chapel ahead of you. Bear right here into the Romsey Road. A short distance further brings you to a T-junction with open fields beyond. Turn right but look almost immediately left for a gate with a stile beside it leading to a footpath over the fields. Cross the stile and follow the path with the hedge on your right towards Kings Farm. Here, surrounded by green rolling farmland, with the damp smell of freshly turned earth from the fields I found it difficult to believe that the Forest Boundary was scarcely half a mile away. Just before Kings Farm, the path leads to a minor road. Turn left down the lane, past the Farm to a wooden footbridge over a stream. This is the Blackwater, once called the Wellow which gave its name to this ancient parish. WELLOW (see Note 2) like so many river names, is from a Celtic word; in this case 'Welewe' meaning 'watery blue'.

Cross the footbridge over this historic stream, and now our walk becomes really lovely. A few yards past the bridge you come to a stile on the right. Cross the stile and follow a raised footpath over the fields towards East Wellow. The tower of the church appears above its surrounding trees on the hill ahead. Go through a gate and over a narrow water meadow — try to see this in early Summer when it is ablaze with Kingcups! Cross another bridge to a deep sunken path that climbs gradually up to the church. Oak tree roots cling to the path's crumbling sides providing sheltered corners for the earliest primroses. At the top you come to the CHURCH OF ST MARGARET (see Note 3), built in the same year that King John signed the Magna Carta, 1215.

A mile east of the church stands Florence Nightingale's home, Embley Park. She made her first attempts to care for the sick in the cottages round about. The house has been much altered, but the library still shows some curious false backs masking a door which were in place in her time. Walk round the church to the porch on the south side and in front of it you will see her grave under a pyramid shaped memorial. At her own request the grave is marked by the initials FN only. As you enter the porch, look up to see one of the original iron bound lamps Florence Nightingale carried at Scutari. The door is from an earlier Saxon building and is a massive construction of solid Forest timber on its long original hinges and dating back to 850 AD! It is covered with nail holes showing where, in the sixteenth century, rats and other vermin were fastened. Catching these animals was quite a profitable business for the Churchwardens paid so much per head. That was probably a lot cheaper than constantly replacing hymn books! There is much to see inside the church too, including the thirteenth century wall paintings which are very well preserved, and fascinating mementos of Florence Nightingale.

Retrace your steps back to West Wellow by the same route. As I came to the top of the sunken path again and looked over the peaceful fields, woods, and water meadows that Florence Nightingale knew so well I thought what a contrast she must have found between this quiet scene and the drama, noise and bloodshed of the Crimea! And I remembered the other conflict she had to face between the life she was expected to lead as a wealthy Victorian lady and her own desire to nurse the wounded and sick. She was between two worlds!

Our second short walk — about three and a half miles round — starts from the other side of the A36 at West Wellow. Walk past the Red Rover Inn over the hill until you see the gravel track I mentioned earlier leading left from the other side of the road. Cross the cattle grid and follow the track along the edge of West Wellow Common. The path climbs a little, then turns sharply left. We leave the gravel track here and keep straight on along the path ahead, past a concrete trig point. From this point you have a wonderful view south over the Forest. The Common, kept bare of trees and shrubs by grazing animals, and edged by a few sparse woods, rolls down to meet the Forest we know — dense massed woods around Bramshaw and Nomansland. Look the other way — back the way you have come — and see the contrast between the open common and the hedged fields and fertile farmlands you have been walking through. Here, on the Common, you find yourself literally between two worlds and it is not difficult to imagine what England looked like in the period before the middle ages when countryside meant nothing but forest rather than the open fields and hillside that it does today.

These Commons around the Forest perimeter, not enclosed within the area of the Royal Forest, were not therefore subject to the Forest laws. The old Saxon belief applied that certain rough grazing round a settlement belonged to all to pasture their animals free of charge, although many Commons were eventually brought into private ownership. The rights that were granted to residents in the Royal Forest: to graze cattle and horses, to gather turves, fuel wood, and turn out their pigs in the pannage season were also practised on the Commons. All sorts of difficulties arose when domestic animals strayed into the Forest and wild ones strayed out of it! To solve some of these, the adjacent Commons were included within the boundaries of the Forest in 1964 so that now the Verderers' by-laws controlling stock operate here too. Plaitford Common, which we shall see later in our walk, was bought by the National Trust.

Our path leads down into a shallow valley. As the heather and gorse is so short, this is a marvellous area to look for wildlife, especially birds. I became increasingly disturbed by the mournful, anxious sounds of a lapwing who evidently considered I was dangerously close to its young. And the stonechats were almost as bad as they scolded me busily from the gorse bushes.

Soon you will see some houses over the Common on the left. This is Canada! Make your way towards the minor road running along the edge of the Common in front of them. You pass a conspicuous white farm and then come to two interesting houses. In the garden of one flies the Canadian flag with its red maple leaf and in the other, the Union Jack! It is believed that this small settlement was made originally by some would-be emigrants to Canada who for some reason decided to make the Forest their home instead. Soon you come to the Canada Common sign, surrounded by a semicircle of gravel on your right. Our path is not very clear at this point, but turn right and walk a few yards from the left hand side of the gravel across the Common to join a good path leading west in our direction. Follow this straight ahead aiming for a belt of woodland. As you come closer to the woods there are many tracks but keep straight ahead, skirting the woods, with the trees on your left, until you come to an outcrop of strange old trees which reach like a finger across your path. They are the familiar Forest stunted and twisted oaks, encircled with holly and wreathed with ivy and honeysuckle. Turn right just before this finger of woodland and walk in a northerly direction for a few yards keeping the wood on your left. You will see a gleam of water over the heath ahead. This is our destination, Sturtmore Pond. Now with your back to the wood, keep straight on following the track to the Pond. This is a lovely, remote stretch of water, surrounded by green lawns and dotted with islands. As I stood by the pond, enclosed by rising slopes of heathland, swifts darted and skimmed ceaselessly over its rippling surface and a heron fished quite unaware in a nearby patch of marsh.

With the Pond on your left, follow the track leading ahead, then bearing left towards a line of pylons. In a few yards, turn right along a crosstrack. Follow this straight ahead towards Canada which you can see over the heath, a little to your right. You could make straight for the village, but to avoid the risk of boggy patches, follow our track until you come to a crosspath. Turn a little right and follow this to Canada. A small chapel is conspicuous as you come closer. Just before a fenced area on the left our way is joined by a path on the left. Turn left along this track which leads back to the Canada Common sign. Turn left along the minor road and repass the Farm, then turn left again to follow our earlier path up the heath to the hill crowned by the trig point. Your car is close by and to catch the Southampton bus, turn right along the A36, past the Red Rover to the bus stop a short distance down the hill by Slab Lane.

Notes for Walk 8

Note 1 *The Red Rover*

I expected to see a coach on the Inn sign as 'The Red Rover' was famous during the coaching days, plying between Salisbury and Southampton. But the sign shows a wily-looking fox!

Note 2 *Wellow*

There is a reference to 'Welewe' in a document as early as 553 AD. There are details of the parish, with the same spelling in the Domesday Book. The parish belonged to King Alfred who left it in his will made some years before his death in 901 AD to his daughter, the warrior princess Ethelfleda. She was known as the Lady of the Mercians and after the death of her husband continued to defend her home in the Midlands from the Danes. But another Ethelfleda, King Alfred's niece, chose a gentler life. She became abbess of the Abbey at Romsey.

Note 3 *East Wellow Church*

This is my favourite church in the whole Forest area. It is a treasure house of interesting things to see which combined with its homely atmosphere explains why Florence Nightingale loved it so much. Built in the early thirteenth century, on the site of an earlier Saxon building, the nave and chancel are unaltered, simple in style with the original slim lancet windows above the alter. There is a delightful hexagonal Jacobean pulpit with back panelling and tester or sounding board. This was found, the vicar told me, in a nearby barn and restored to the church in 1907. The nave and chancel are decorated with some fine thirteenth century wall paintings. As you open the south door you see St Christopher — the patron saint of travellers. He is carrying the Christ child of course but in his free hand he holds his eel spear to catch his supper on the way! An ancient musket fastened to one of the roof timbers in the chancel tells a sad tale. It was fixed there by its owner as a warning against the careless use of firearms after the accidental killing of a maid by a fellow servant. A print of Florence Nightingale as a girl — she is very attractive — hangs in the south aisle and there are more mementoes of her in the south window including a small cross made of bullets brought back from the Crimea. The Parish Registers have been preserved in the Church since 1570 and contain some fascinating entries. In 1665 the parishioners were asked to collect for 'two men of ye Ile of Wite, taken prisoners in Turkey'. But entries show troubles much nearer home. The next month 7s and 9d was collected for 'ye poore distressed with ye Pestilence'. A reminder that the great plague of that year was widespread.

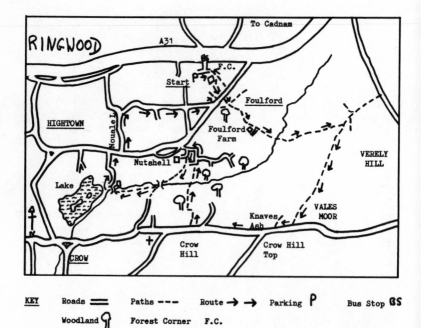

KEY   Roads ═══   Paths ---   Route → →   Parking P   Bus Stop BS

Woodland ♀   Forest Corner F.C.

Scale (miles)

½   1

Above the Avon Valley:
A Forest Panorama

This walk is about five miles round, and you really will have the Forest at your feet! You follow an ancient greenway along one of the Forest's highest ridges of moorland and enjoy wonderful views as you walk. To the south, woods and heaths ripple towards the horizon formed by the curving blue line of the Isle of Wight hills. To the north-west, where the Forest trees edge the hillside above the Avon valley, you look down over the lush watermeadows threaded by the silver ribbon of the Avon. Allow a good half-day to give time to enjoy all this beauty.

Our starting point is Forest Corner, a bus stop beside the A31 on the hill above Ringwood, about a mile from Picket Post. Opposite, a minor road runs north to Poulner and Hangersley. Driving from Southampton along the A31 look for the sign indicating this minor road on the right and on the left you will see a track leading over a cattle grid. Turn in here and park beside the track. Coming by bus from Southampton, catch the Bournemouth bus which is routed through Ringwood. You have a pleasant, if rather long journey across the Forest to its western boundary at Forest Corner. By the bus stop I saw a memorial which delighted me. There is a seat and a carved stone in memory of BARON EVERSLEY (see Note 1), a pioneer in the preservation of areas of outstanding natural beauty.

Cross the cattle grid and follow the footpath sign over the Common. As I walked in a strong westerly wind I experienced what is known in the Forest as 'clulberry weather', now a hint of rain, now a moment of dazzling sunshine, the cloud shadows dancing over the heath bringing constantly changing colours and contrasts. The path runs by a hedge round a white house. Bear right along the path and a short way over the heath until you come to a minor road which runs to Ringwood through Hightown. Cross straight over it and follow the footpath sign over the heath ahead in the direction of a cluster of cottages called Foulford. In front of you runs the high ridge followed by the greenway we are to take. Our path dips into a valley beside woods of old firs and beeches below the ridge. You now walk through an old oak wood, hidden in the valley, the spreading branches of the trees wreathed in blackthorn. Pass a Forest farm with a thatched barn on the right then walk through more oak woods down to a stream. We cross this little stream again as it flows, copper coloured, to meet the Avon, later in our walk. Cross the bridge and climb up the heath track ahead towards the top of the ridge. As you climb, the country unfolds with spreading views all around you. Behind is the valley with its sunny oak woods, and away to the west opens the Avon valley framed by soft waves of blue hills. I was enjoying the view when I saw to my surprise a herd of fallow deer within a few feet of me. I had walked right past them — they had not noticed me nor I them. I counted sixteen and so perfectly did their plain dun coloured winter coats match the heathland that without their white rumps I believe I would not have seen them, close as they were. In Summer their coats are golden brown with white spots, in Winter they change to this darker shade that makes them almost invisible in woods as well as on heaths. Fallow deer in parks can have coats of either shade but do not change in this way.

As you reach flatter ground at the top of the ridge, you come to the wide greenway. This beautiful, banked route runs the whole length of the hillside over Poor Man's Common where we are standing to Picket Post, a little to our left. It commands a marvellous view over all the surrounding countryside and is possibly a very old track indeed. Turn right and walk along this lovely path. To the left is the Forest with Burley Hill Fort rising dramatically from the heath and in front the Avon valley. A smaller hill on your left is Verely, a reminder of the Forest's smuggling days. This ridge way was a favourite smuggler's route from Highcliffe where goods were landed, across the Forest to Picket Post where there were underground cellars for storage. A woman called Lovey Warne took an active part in these proceedings. Wearing a conspicuous red cloak she would stand on Verely Hill to warn the smugglers if the Revenue men were about. I found it hard to believe that anyone could use so lofty a route to smuggle anything along but I believe I found the answer. A few yards to the left of the raised greenway, running parallel with it, is a deep sunken path, wide enough for men and pack animals. Choose an area where the gorse has been burnt to have a look along it. The path is deep enough to conceal people from even close observers. A similar smuggler's track crosses Ridley Wood, a mile east of Picket Post.

The path falls sharply to bring you off the ridge down to the minor road that runs through Burley Street towards Ringwood and Crow. Turn right to walk on the Heath beside the road past Knaves Ash house and Crow Hill top. We are now crossing the Forest boundary and this border area is full of interest. The large holes on the slopes beyond Knaves Ash, which were used as a rifle range, are said to have been dug originally as shelter by Cromwell's troops on their way through this hostile part of the country from Dorset to London. CROW HILL (see Note 2) has been a settlement since the eleventh century and was once quite a busy place, the villagers making bricks and knitted gloves.

Follow the minor road for about three quarters of a mile until you see a footpath sign on your right, leading into a spinney. Turn right and follow the sign which brings you to a splendid path bordered by tall oaks. When you come to a field bear left along the edge then right beside a wood to a bridge with a white hand rail. This takes you over the stream we crossed earlier in the oak wood. Climb the path ahead through more oaks and beeches. I walked through a carpet of white wood anemones. Each delicate flower poised above its rosette of leaves moves with every breath of wind, no wonder they are also called windflowers. You come out of the wood to follow a path beside some houses. Cross a stile, pass the houses on your right and keep straight on along the gravel track ahead until you come to a road. Turn left here along the lane. (Ignore the footpath straight ahead). A few yards down the lane you will see a minor road ahead of you, running to Hightown. Just before the road look for a sign 'To Nutshell' on your left. This is a right of way although I noticed the footpath sign was broken. Turn left down here for a few yards. A drive curves away right for 'Nutshell' and our way is straight on over the grass towards a gate immediately ahead. A stile beside the gate takes you into another oak shaded lane. Our way bears right, over a plank bridge, then left along the side of a meadow and down to a stream. Now the path turns right to follow the streamside which is a paradise for wild flowers. The little stream twists and turns beneath its shading trees carving peninsulas and islands covered in primroses and violets. We leave the stream as it turns south to run almost parallel with the Avon for a while. Go past a concrete building on the right and over a stile to a gravel track beside a lake. Turn right and follow the track uphill to meet the minor road running through Hightown. Across the road, a little to your right, you will see some cottages, tucked cosily under the hillside bordering the Avon valley. Follow the road for a few yards until you come to a lane leading left past the cottages called Nouale Lane. Follow this pleasant lane as it takes you slightly uphill towards the A31. Across the flat meadows bordering the Avon is Ringwood, the tower of its old church now close to us. When the lane bears right more steeply uphill, look for a wide track leading from the lane on the right with a bridleway sign. On the map this is about halfway between the minor road at Hightown and the A31. We need to follow this back towards Foulford to pick up our original path over the common to return to Forest Corner. So turn right following the Bridleway sign, climbing a little along a shallow valley. Soon the gravel track becomes better defined and we pass a mixture of modern houses and old Forest cottages to join the Hightown road again further north, just before the Forest boundary.

Cross the cattle grid on your left and walk beside the road over the heath until you come to the point where you crossed the road at the beginning of the walk. Ignore the first footpath sign you see on the right. Turn left at the second footpath sign and retrace the route to the hedge round the white house. Follow the path back to the cattle grid beside the A31 at Forest Corner. To catch a return bus to Southampton, cross the road to the stop in front of a market garden.

Notes for Walk 9

Note 1 *Baron Eversley*
He fought a thirty year campaign through the law courts of England to resist the enclosure of common lands during the latter half of the nineteenth century. In 1864 he launched the Commons Preservation Society which succeeded in establishing a principle in law recognising the right of all to

enjoy the countryside with access to famous viewpoints. He fought for the preservation of footpaths and public rights of way and in 1894 published an account of this work under the title 'Commons, Forests and Footpaths'. It is right that so fine a man should be remembered here on this lovely hillside.

Note 2 *Crow Hill*

A primitive form of brick making took place here; the clay being dug from a pond in the Autumn and trodden with bare feet in the Spring when the bricks were made. They were baked in kilns heated by gorse from the Forest. Gloves were also made here and one of the present inhabitants remembers helping her mother to knit them. She was only five, just old enough to knit the straightforward plain and purl cuffs!

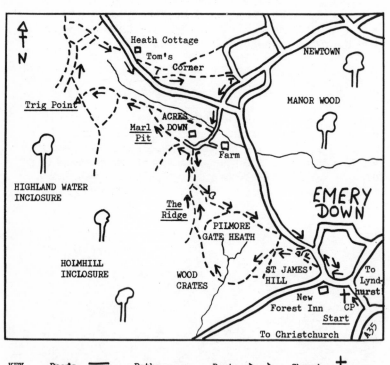

N

Heath Cottage

Tom's

Corner

NEWTOWN

MANOR WOOD

Trig Point

ACRES
DOWN

Marl
Pit

Farm

EMERY
DOWN

HIGHLAND WATER
INCLOSURE

The
Ridge

PILMORE
GATE HEATH

HOLMHILL
INCLOSURE

WOOD
CRATES

ST JAMES'
HILL

To
Lynd-
hurst

New
Forest Inn

CP

Start

To Christchurch

A35

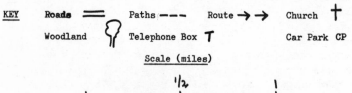

KEY   Roads ═══   Paths ---   Route → →   Church †

Woodland   Telephone Box T   Car Park CP

Scale (miles)

½   1

Ridge Walk from Emery Down

Ridge walks are rare in the Forest, being generally low-lying, but when they do occur they give us rare insights into the Forest's beauty; its contrasting shades of woodlands and wide expanses of quiet heaths. This ridge walk, only two miles from the Forest capital, Lyndhurst, is my favourite. There is no difficulty in finding it — no trackless wastes to cross — but it will lead you to the real heart of this wonderful Forest. The distance round is about seven and a half miles but I will suggest also a shorter return route which reduces the distance to about four miles. Allow a full day for the longer walk.

We start among the glorious woods north-west of Lyndhurst from Swan Green, the hamlet on the A35 Bournemouth road, just west of the Forest capital. It's so close you can walk from Lyndhurst or catch the bus from Southampton. Walk up the road towards Bournemouth for a few yards then turn right at Swan Green along the road to Emery Down. If you arrive by car, park in the Swan Green car park which is on the left of the road to Emery Down. Follow the road to the top of the hill overlooking Emery Down. The scattered houses of the village appear dotted along the hillside; their gardens making colourful oases among the dips and hollows. You pass a lane on the right in front of Honeysuckle Cottage called Silver Street.

Our road through the village turns left to pass the church and a group of almshouses built round a courtyard. They are all built of the same warm red brick. Christ Church, Emery Down, was built in 1864 from designs by William Butterfield. It was the gift of Admiral Boultbee who also endowed the almshouses which are known locally as 'Boultbee's cottages'.

Before the junction with the Ringwood road you pass the New Forest Inn. In the early 1700's a caravan stood on this site having claimed squatters' rights. Now the caravan forms the front lounge porchway and the Inn is built either side of it. Bear right in front of the Inn, following the road signposted Stoney Cross and Fritham. The village here is so pretty, its houses framed by Forest trees and encircled by buttercup-filled meadows, that it is easy to understand why it has always been popular with writers and artists. The novelist, Mary Braddon, lived here at Annesley Bank. In 1862 her novel 'Lady Audley's Secret' caused a sensation, selling nearly a million copies.

After about a quarter of a mile, opposite a lane on the right, you will come to a turning on the left, just past a letter box. Turn left and after a few yards the track divides. Follow the right hand track which soon comes to a white footpath leading across the Forest lawn ahead. This brings you to the woods around the northern edge of St James' Hill. As you come to the edge of the woods, bear left at a fork into the trees. Cross a more open area to another fork in the path. Again bear left. Shortly you come to a gate leading to a woodland track skirting the hill. Follow this lovely way through old woods of oaks and beeches, holly and silver birches. The first time I came this way the trees had all the fresh green of May. Dappled sunlight fell on glades of heather and bilberry bushes among a glorious tangle of russet bracken fronds. I was contemplating all this when a large fox came trotting round a curve in the path straight towards me. It would be difficult to say who was most surprised! He stopped, small triangular face alert, green eyes gleaming, red-brown body motionless. Then, with no sigh of alarm or a moment's panic, he turned, his wide brush sweeping the path, and trotted round me to rejoin the path a few yards further on. There was no doubt in his mind who was the intruder.

This delightful path takes you all round the base of ST JAMES' HILL (see Note 1). There are very few hills like this in the Forest, isolated, over three hundred feet high and still retaining a thick gravel capping.

As you walk you will notice an inclosure boundary fence on your right. Our path leads to the fence. Cross over and you will see a good path beside it. Turn right and walk beside the fence for a few yards, then follow the path as it bears left among the trees at Wood Crates. Now you can see our objective clearly, a high ridge of heath and gorse covered moorland rising ahead a little to your right. Our way runs over the valley through a fringe of trees. Then, just before a thicker belt of woodland, the way forks. Go right here into Wood Crates. Cross a stream, a tributary of Highland Water, and you come to another fork. Bear right again so that the high, smooth ridge of moorland is now directly ahead. Our way is clear, over the heath in the valley, then winding to the top of the ridge through low gorse and holly and silver birches. Climb to the top to find yourself in a wonderful spot. You stand high on the heath, at the beginning of the ridge. All around you spread billowing waves of woodlands. The dark pines of Highland Water contrast with the bright greens of the oaks and beeches of Holmill and Wood Crates, St James and Lyndhurst Hills. There is a glimpse of Southampton, framed by these massed woods and far away on the horizon, the soft blue of the Isle of Wight hills. This is a place to rest the spirit.

Walk across the ridge to meet a crosstrack. Now turn right so that you follow the crest with Highland Water valley and Inclosure on your left. After about a quarter of a mile you will see a track leading along the valley over Pilmore Gate Heath on your right. At this point, if you prefer the shorter walk, turn right along this path. It leads straight back to the minor road running from Stoney Cross to Emery Down. At the road, turn right to walk a short distance to Emery Down.

For our longer walk, keep straight on past this right turn, and walk down the hill through a wood to a lane beside Acres Down House. Look across the lane for a sign 'Acres Down House and Cottage only'. That is our way. With the House and Cottage on your right, follow the path leading past them over the heath. A little to the left of our path a tall stand of pines shade an old marl pit. 'MARLING' (see Note 2) was an ancient method of fertilising land by spreading over it material dug from pits like this.

Our way winds over a narrow strip of heathland, bearing left towards the edge of a pine wood. Follow the path until it meets a crosstrack. The pine wood is close on the left and by the gate into it is a white concrete trig point. Turn right at the crosstrack, cross a few yards of heath, then right again towards an old oak and beech wood. Our way is through the glades at the edge of the wood, shaded by massive trees and deep in mast. Ahead you will see the minor road running from Stoney Cross to Emery Down. Before you meet the road, you come to another crosstrack. Turn right and follow this track until it eventually meets the minor road opposite Heath Cottage. Cross the road and turn right beside the road and walk for about a quarter of a mile in the direction of Emery Down. Ignore the first public footpath sign you see on the left but take the next turn left for Tom's Corner. Now look for our footpath leading left over the green. Follow this path as it becomes a deep lane leading down a fertile valley of small fields and fruit trees. You are in the farming country which surrounds Minstead. I was intrigued by the old farm machines laid up on the grass beside the track. The path meets a lane at Newtown. Some thatched and half-timbered cottagese here belie the truth of the name! Turn right along the lane for a few yards to a phone box on the corner, then right again. The lane brings you quickly back to the minor road again, the one from Stoney Cross to Emery Down. Cross the road and immediately opposite is a lane leading downhill. Follow the lane, cross the stream, Bartley Water, and up the road to rejoin our earlier route at Acres Down. Follow our original track — it led us off the ridge — as it climbs through the woods, from Acres Down, and proceeds ahead. As you reach the top and the path levels onto the heath, look for the path now on your left that I mentioned earlier as the way back to Emery Down. Close at hand it is not very distinct but further away you will see it more clearly leading down then along the valley over Pilmore Gate Heath. To the right of the path the heath slopes up to the ridge and to the left a belt of trees divides an area of farmland from our valley. Turn left following this path towards Emery Down. At a junction bear left into a gravelled lane leading to the minor road just above the village. Turn right and walk back through the village to Swan Green. The car park is on your right or you can catch the bus back to Southampton on the main A35 road opposite.

Notes for Walk 10

Note 1 *St James' Hill*
The gravel made it valuable. On an old map of 1789 it is called 'gravel hill' and old diggings remain on the top. Until recent times all Forest roads were gravel. I am told that the main road from Ashurst through Lyndhurst was gravelled up to the

beginning of the second world war. But in former days the less important pathways through the Forest were mud tracks. Coaches and carriages had to be preceded by armed postillions with a guide. At night large circular horn lanterns holding three candles each known as 'moons' were fixed to poles and attached to the stirrups of the postillions.

Note 2 *Marling*

This was a skilled craft with a host of technical terms, songs, customs and sayings attached to it. Two sayings I have heard are 'he that marls moss shall have no loss' and 'he that marls clay flings all away'. Gangs of marlers went from farm to farm, one of whom was chosen as 'Lord of the Soil'. Passers-by were asked for money and at the end of the week there was a celebration at the local Inn. When a whole area was finished, everyone joined in — marlers, farmworkers, neighbours and tenants — there were drinks for all, songs, dancing and no doubt a good supper as well!

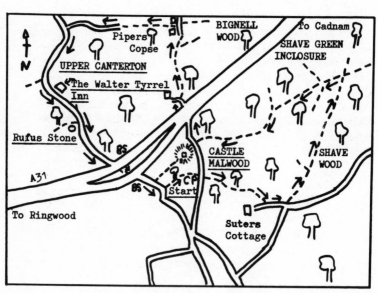

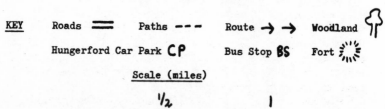

KEY   Roads ▬▬   Paths ‑‑‑   Route →→   Woodland 🌳

Hungerford Car Park CP   Bus Stop BS   Fort ☼

Scale (miles)

½   1

Secrets of the Forest

The New Forest with its nine hundred years of history has more than its share of secrets. This walk, mainly through old woodlands, explores the most mysterious part of the Forest. Our starting point has the intriguing name of Castle Malwood. Close by, an event took place which still puzzles historians. Only the Forest knows the real answer! This was the death of William the Conqueror's favourite son, William Rufus on August 2, 1100. While out hunting in Canterton Glen an arrow, allegedly shot by a nobleman Walter Tyrrel, pierced his heart. An accident? Or was it murder? (see Note 1). We visit the spot where he fell now marked by the Rufus Stone. Tradition also tells us that the night before, William Rufus had slept at CASTLE MALWOOD (see Note 2). Historians may differ over the facts concerning his death and the exact spot where he fell may not be known exactly, but what is so exciting for us today is that the Forest remains much as he saw it. He would still feel quite at home among the woods and glades we walk through.

If you glance at the map you will see that our route divides into two walks so if you prefer you could walk through Shave Woods one day and through Canterton Glen another. The distance round the combined walks is about six and a half miles; four miles through Shave Woods and about two and a half to visit the countryside round Canterton Glen. Allow a good half day for the whole walk.

Castle Malwood is beside the A31, Southampton-Ringwood road. If you are driving from Southampton about a mile and a half past the Cadnam roundabout turn left down a minor road signposted Minstead and Lyndhurst. After quarter of a mile the road divides. Take the narrow road left and a few yards further on pull into Hungerford Car Park. There is a lane to the car park directly from the A31, but as (at the time of writing) it is not signposted, it is safer to take the slightly longer route I suggest. If you come on the bus from Southampton, you pass the minor road and stop close to the small lodge at the entrance to Castle Malwood. Walk back to the minor road signposted Minstead and Lyndhurst, and follow it right. Ignore the first lane on your left and look for a second smaller lane leading left, just before the Minstead sign. It is marked 'Hollybrae'. Turn left down this lane and when a track goes right for 'Hollybrae', carry straight on down the hill. The path brings you quickly to Hungerford Car Park, the starting point beside Castle Malwood.

Encircling the hill to the left you will see a deep ditch and embankment. This explains the 'Castle', a name given in the Forest to the remains of Iron Age hill forts (see Walk Seven. Note 4). Within the embankment stands Malwood Lodge, built in 1884 in neo-Tudor style for Sir William Harcourt, then Gladstone's Home Secretary. It is on the site of a former simple Forest lodge and documentary evidence proves that in 1358 a lodge called Hardebourgh stood here. So there seems no reason to disbelieve the tradition that William Rufus feasted and slept here the night before his death.

Cross the road from Hungerford car park and follow the footpath ahead into Shave Woods. These are interesting old woods, with here and there among the oaks and beeches, some ancient pollards. Pollards are mostly over three hundred years old. Their main trunks have been shortened while quite young so that now they spread many twisting, curving trunks in all directions making shaded glades beneath them. I stopped to look more closely at a much smaller tree, a lime, with silvery green leaves furry to touch. LIME TREES (see Note 3) like this one are fairly rare in the Forest and when you do see them they make a delightful cool contrast with the oaks and beeches. In Summer bunches of still tightly closed flowers hang like small tassels among the leaves.

Soon you come to a more open area with green lawns dotted by fine oaks ahead. Cross the lawns to a gravel track. On the hillside to the right are a few houses and cottages and a large grey building, Minstead Lodge. Our way bears left past a sign 'Suters cottage only' to meet a minor road. Walk straight ahead along the road for a few yards to the corner where the road bends sharply right. Leading left from the corner is our path. Follow it uphill towards Shave Green Inclosure. Our way bears left into the wood under the arching boughs of tall unpollarded beeches which meet over your head so that you feel you are walking in some vast green roofed cathedral. Follow the path as it leads over a hill deeper into the shade of these beautiful trees. In a clearing I was delighted by a familiar, age-old Forest scene: a tiny spindly-legged foal nudging close to his mother for comfort in a world still too new for him!

Keep straight on over all crosstracks. You may have to pick your way round the occasional fallen tree. As they are so large this may mean quite a lengthy detour. Looking at these mighty beeches rising from their deep carpet of russet leaves, it is surprising to recall that this area of the Forest, between Romsey and Lyndhurst, very nearly became farmland during the reign of Queen Anne. Daniel Defoe,, author of 'Robinson Crusoe' and an indefatigable traveller who published his 'Tour Through the Whole Island of Great Britain' in 1726, suggested that refugees from the Palatine should be settled here (see Note 4).

The path becomes a wide greenway, fenced at both sides leading between new beech woods sheltered by pine 'nurses'. When you come to a gravel track, turn left and go through a gate. Here you find another of the Forest's hidden secrets! Standing each side of the track ahead are magnificent Douglas Firs, their tall soaring trunks a rough, flaking reddish-brown and their great sweeping branches sighing in every breath of wind. From the gate, walk between these wonderful trees along the edge of Shave Green Inclosure. Go straight over all crosstracks and again when the gravel track turns right, keep straight on down the grassy path ahead following the line of the Douglas Firs. You come to a plantation of young pines on the left with several deer hides. Deer love to browse on young pines and sure enough two deer ran out of it and over my path. I was interested to see they were red deer hinds, not numerous in the Forest. Dark red-brown in colour, not as graceful as the roe and without the fallow's distinctive white patch, their chief beauty is I think their small, daintily-formed heads. Their large prominent ears flopped as they ran back into cover. Go through a gate and follow the path as it bears left to bring you back through Shave Woods. Our way is roughly parallel with the A31 which you cannot see although you will hear the sound of its traffic. Just past a large open area on the left, our path bears right, uphill before turning right. You will see the embankments of Castle Malwood fort ahead. You come out of the woods onto the narrow road running immediately in front of the fort where we began our walk. If you would like to finish here, turn left and walk a few yards down the road to Hungerford car park which is on your right. To catch the bus back to Southampton, retrace your steps across the car park to the Minstead road. Turn right for the A31. Cross the westbound carriage way and follow the footpath over the central reservation. You will see the bus stop on the other side of the eastbound carriage way a few yards to your right.

To continue our longer walk, turn right when you come to the narrow road in front of Castle Malwood fort. Walk the few yards to the A31. Cross the road and follow the track immediately ahead, leading downhill through the trees. When the track bears left towards a house, keep straight on along the edge of the woods towards Canterton Manor. You leave the woods to cross clearings dotted with small silver birches. In about half a mile look left for glimpses of houses among the trees. You come to a crosstrack so turn left along it towards the houses. The path is not distinct here, but you can see the houses clearly. Cross the wide green lawn to the lane running in front of the cottages. Dreaming peacefully beneath the shelter of the Forest oaks, this part of Canterton looks as remote as it was in the days of William Rufus. The name 'Canterton' (meaning 'the village of the Kentish men' or the Jutes) recalls that it was Jutish tribes who first settled in the New Forest after the departure of the Roman legions.

Between the cottages on your left you will see a wide greenway which leads to Piper's Copse. The Copse is privately owned but this path is a right of way. Follow the path left, down to a stream and into the copse. The track through the trees has sunk between high banks entwined with tree roots which make such perfect homes for wild flowers. The path leads to a lane which meets a minor road. Turn left here and follow the minor road towards Upper Canterton. You pass the Walter Tyrrel Inn on the left. Just past the Inn, turn left and walk round the green. You will see a New Forest cottage with a real old world garden; the sort of cottage I felt could well be haunted by the ghost

90

dog of the Forest. He was Walter Tyrrel's dog and is able to rush in and out of houses through the walls! He was a much more effective threat for naughty Forest children than 'Boney'!

Now as you walk back towards the main road you come to the famous Rufus Stone a little to the right of the lane. It looks rather like an iron-encased trig point, shaped like a small tower with four sides. On one side we read 'Here stood the oak tree on which an arrow shot by Sir Walter Tyrrel at a stag glanced and struck King William II, surnamed Rufus, on the breast of which he instantly died on the second day of August Anno 1100.' This most detested of Kings was left where he fell to be found by a charcoal burner called Purkiss who took his body on his cart to Winchester along a route still called the King's road.

From the Rufus Stone walk up the hill to the A31. The bus stop for Southampton is on your left. To return to Hungerford car park cross the road and follow the minor road signposted Minstead and Lyndhurst retracing your route at the beginning of our walk.

Notes for Walk 11

Note 1 *Death of William Rufus*

According to the contemporary chroniclers William Rufus, now King, was hunting with his younger brother Henry, his good friend Fitzhamon, and Walter Tyrrel who had just arrived from Normandy where the King's enemies had been outlawed. As the sun was setting the King found himself alone with Tyrrel. A stag bounded past. 'Shoot!' cried the King, when his arrow only slightly wounded it. Tyrrel shot and his arrow pierced Rufus's heart. He died immediately. Tyrrel fled to Normandy, but no pursuit was organised. Henry made straight to Winchester where he secured the national treasury, then continued to London where he persuaded the Bishop to crown him King on 5 August — only three days after his brother's death! Haste was necessary as Henry had another brother, Duke Robert, to whom he had promised allegiance, but who happened to be conveniently in Normandy at the time. Fitzhamon, the fourth member of the hunting party, loyally rushed to Normandy to tell Robert what had happened. If it was murder, you can take your pick among a host of suspects. The Saxons hated their Norman Kings of course but even his own countrymen detested Rufus. The clergy, rich and powerful, objected to his choice of favourites, the barons disliked him for extending his Forest Laws over their lands. Then there were the allies of his brothers who had their eyes on the crown. They were not the sons of William the Conqueror for nothing! Evidence does seem to point to Henry as being the villain of the piece. If you would like to pursue this remarkable who-dun-it further you should read Duncan Grinnel Milne's book 'The Killing of William Rufus'. Tyrrel protested he was innocent even on his deathbed!

Note 2 *Rufus at Castle Malwood*
The King ate and drank regally — probably too well. The Saxon chroniclers (prone to exaggeration concerning the hated Normans) tell us that he awoke suddenly to see a vision of a stream of blood — his own — pouring from heaven and clouding the daylight. Next day monks came and gave him more warnings. He would not have improved his standing with his English subjects when he told them: 'Am I an Englishman, who puts faith in the dreams of every old woman?' He fortified himself with a few more drinks then went out hunting, never to return.

Note 3 *Lime Trees in the Forest*
So this was not one of our native limes whose fruits are not pendulous. It was probably a descendant of an import from Holland. Lime trees, like tulips, were enthusiastically imported from that country in the seventeenth century, and planted throughout England. Limes were very useful trees. Most of Grinling Gibbons carving was in lime wood, and the bark can be made into ropes, nets, mats, even clothes! So when Lyndhurst was first settled — in the Domesday Book it is Linhest, wood of lime trees — the villagers would have made good use of their trees.

Note 4 *Daniel Defoe's plan*
In 1709, ten thousand refugees from the Rhenish Palatinate came to England to escape the miseries of war and oppression in their own country. They were housed in huts on the heaths near London. Some went abroad to found a settlement in Pennsylvania, but the only rational plan for their care was proposed by Defoe. He suggested that certain selected families should be given areas of barren land — like this part of the

Forest — so that they would employ others and that in time communities would be formed with churches, schools and shops. Defoe's far-sighted plans even included a health service! It was a splendid plan, like so many of Defoe's economic theories, but came to nothing as Lord Treasurer Godolphin who approved of it, soon lost his office.